I never tire of watching Robert Redford and his two children when they visit my restaurant. They always order Beef Sadea and seem to enjoy the process of cooking, each with his own hibachi, as much as they do the actual eating.

It is because making Beef Sadea is like a mini-barbecue that it is such a delightful family or party dish. Adults and children all seem to enjoy the do-it-yourself cooking . . . as long as they don't have to worry about the dirty dishes!

Barbecued Beef
🔄 Siu Nagu Yoke 🔄

HAVE READY:

½ pound top sirloin, cut into 16 bite-size pieces

1 tablespoon dark Chinese soy sauce

1 teaspoon light Chinese soy sauce

1 1½" slice fresh ginger root,

2 cloves crushed garlic (optional)

1 teaspoon red cooking wine

½ teaspoon sugar

METHOD:

Prepare a marinade of the soy sauces, ginger root, garlic, wine and sugar, and marinate the sirloin pieces overnight, then broil in an oven for 3 minutes on each side. Serve with colored toothpicks as hors d'oeuvres.

Allows 4 pieces per person when serving four.

Madame Wu's
Art of
Chinese
Cooking

To my grandfather,
from whom I received
the precious gift of love.

Contents

VEGETABLE DISHES

EGG DISHES

RICE and NOODLE DISHES

I was born to a merchant family in Kiukiang, a city on the Yangtse River in the province of Kiangsi, where my grandfather owned a department store and a small bank. As was the custom in old China, the girls in the upper-class families were not permitted into the kitchen. Instead, they were tutored in the Chinese classics, taught to do delicate embroidery and learned the manners of proper young ladies.

The kitchen in our home was very large, and near the door was a stove made of earth. On it rested a wok, an iron cooking pot, that was almost as big in circumference as an American card table. The stove was wood-burning and the smoke coming from it made the kitchen very dirty, not an appropriate place to be visited by well-mannered little girls.

My grandfather was a gourmet who loved to cook. I would hide near the door and peek through into the kitchen to watch him while he was cooking. Without realizing it, I was learning the basic principles of food preparation. Although we had a first cook and a second cook (the first does the cooking, the second the washing and cutting), my grandfather actually was the chef, preparing our food most of the time. He enjoyed going to the market to do his own shopping, choosing exactly what he needed, always looking for the foods that were my favorites. The Chinese people do not show affection by kissing and hugging, but rather by preparing special dishes for those they want to please.

For example, he knew how much I liked fresh water crabs. So as soon as they appeared on the market, he would buy them, prepare them and place that particular dish in front of me on the lazy susan which centered our round table. I have wonderful memories of those years in my grandfather's house.

When it was time for me to go to college, I was sent to the United States in order to attend Columbia Teacher's College in New York. During that period I married a young engineer I had known in Hong Kong who had just received his post-graduate degree from the Massachusetts Institute of Technology.

All of a sudden I was called upon to put my theories of cooking into practice. But instead of the familiar wood-burning stove, I had to master the art of cooking on a gas stove. Every time I turned on the gas, I was terrified that I would burn myself. Gradually, though, my enthusiasm for duplicating the special dishes my husband and I were served at friends' homes or at Chinese restaurants helped me to overcome my fear of the stove, and slowly I began to accumulate a file of my own recipes.

I also had a stroke of good fortune which furthered my cooking skills. When my daughter was two years old, we went to visit my mother-in-law in Hong Kong and her going-away present to me was a Chinese housekeeper whom she had personally trained. She was a wonderful cook, knowledgeable in all forms of Oriental cuisine, and I learned a great deal from her.

Because my husband came from a diplomatic family (his grandfather was the co-founder of the Republic of China with Dr. Sun Yat Sen, and the first Ambassador to the United States), we did a great deal of entertaining in our home. The preparation of elaborate Chinese dinners soon became very easy for me.

When our three children were in their teens, we made another visit to Hong Kong. While I was there I spent a considerable time looking into the operation of Chinese restaurants, and upon our return, I announced to my husband that I wanted to open a restaurant of my own. I don't think he took me very seriously at first, for he made no objections. He was convinced, however, when I found a suitable place near our home in West Los Angeles, and six months later my first Wu's Garden was opened.

The restaurant was a success from the first day it opened. We attracted the leaders of the entertainment, scientific, professional and business worlds. The food must have been the major attraction since we did not have a cocktail license, booths or carpets . . . just simple tables and chairs.

Two years later we expanded, adding a cocktail bar and complementing the food with a more elegant decor. Several more years were to pass before I opened the new and more expansive Madame Wu's Garden in Santa Monica; and, although I credit the cuisine for our continuing growth, I am not only aware of but also grateful for the publicity which follows our celebrity clientele.

Since President Nixon's historic trip to Peking, interest in anything Chinese has expanded a hundredfold. Almost a quarter of a century has passed since the bamboo screen shielded China from the world's view. Now it has been moved to one side just enough to tantalize Westerners with glimpses of a forbidden land and a people whose culture goes back more than 4000 years.

Highlighting the press dispatches during and immediately following the Presidential visit were descriptions of each course served at the gala banquet given by Premier Chou En-lai for President Nixon. Again this is understandable, since the Chinese have recognized cooking as an art form for thousands of years.

Following the China trip, the newspapers and magazines printed as many different ways to prepare Peking Duck as there were reporters and cooking editors to write them. Since I have featured Peking Duck ever since I first opened my restaurant, I was sincerely disturbed over the confused and confusing versions of the recipe. Many were so complicated that even a master chef, I'm sure, would have some difficulty in following the directions.

As a direct result, I spent considerable time developing my personal Peking Duck recipe in answer to numerous requests; and this growing interest in Chinese food was reflected not only in our increasing business but in the desire of both my old as well as new customers to prepare these dishes in their own kitchens.

There was only one answer—to give a series of cooking classes. For the first series of classes, there were some 600 applicants but room for only 60 students. Someone once wrote that imitation is the sincerest form of flattery, and the fact that my students went home after each lesson and successfully duplicated what I had taught them gave me great pleasure.

Only then did I seriously start considering writing the cookbook I had so often been urged to do, for I knew I would never have time to give Chinese cooking lessons to all those who wanted them.

One final experience convinced me to write this book. My daughter Loretta was brought up in the old-fashioned Chinese manner, which meant she never learned to cook. Shortly after she married, she gave a family dinner party, following recipes step by step from an American cookbook. The dinner was a great success, and it made me realize that an up-to-date Chinese cookbook would be helpful to the newly-married Chinese girl such as Loretta as well as her American counterparts.

In order to insure the accuracy of every recipe, each was carefully tested in my cooking classes, as well as in private sessions. For my readers who live in areas where it might be difficult to buy certain ingredients, substitutions are suggested.

Incidentally, I had more men students than women in my recipe-testing classes, which shouldn't be surprising, I suppose, since the world's greatest chefs—French, Chinese or Italian —have always been men. I think there may be another reason: if the Women's Liberation Movement continues to grow, these far-sighted would-be chefs have already insured their self-preservation!

These last cooking class students have encouraged me greatly in the preparation of this book, and here I would like to thank my two good friends, Paul Marsh and Charlotte Leigh-Taylor, who helped me with research and with the editing of the recipes in an understandable style. Because Chinese chefs rarely use measurements or printed recipes, without the assistance of Mr. Marsh and Mrs. Leigh-Taylor, this book would never have come into being.

Finally, I trust that I have made the recipes so

complete and understandable that you, like I who never set foot in a kitchen until I was in my teens, can now become accomplished in the art of Chinese cooking!

Sylvia Wu

Madame Sylvia Wu
Santa Monica, California
December, 1973

The Schools of Chinese Cooking

Much importance was placed on the preparation of even our daily meals when I was growing up in China. From marketing to serving, the art of cooking was a highly revered skill. This was true of even the most isolated areas where the peasants could make delectable dishes out of the most meager ingredients.

The differences in climate and geography were responsible for the five distinct schools of Chinese cooking: Peking, also known as Mandarin (northern and coastal regions); Szechwan (central and inland); Shanghai (eastern and coastal); Fukien (southeastern and coastal); and Cantonese (southern and coastal).

Fish of both the fin and shell varieties are found in recipes from all five schools, since much of China borders on three seas (Yellow, East China and South China Seas) and there are three major rivers which run through the land (Yellow, Yangtze and Pearl Rivers). Because the Chinese had long perfected the art of drying and preserving fish, even the inland areas could obtain dried fish.

The word "Peking" means "northern capital," and because it was the location of the Imperial Palace for several centuries, chefs from all of China were recruited to serve their famous dishes to the reigning court. The most well-known of these is Peking Duck.

The staple food of Peking is not rice but wheat flour, which explains the widespread use of noodles in the north. Spring rolls also originated there, as did the pancake which is served with the Peking Duck. It resembles the Mexican tortilla, and is made from fine, soft white flour.

The large province of Szechwan is mainly mountainous. Inland, it has a hot, humid climate. The people of Szechwan eat very highly spiced food which probably makes them perspire and thus live more comfortably in this climate. The Szechwan pepper is native to this area.

A popular Szechwan dish is Kung Bow Chicken (diced chicken with hot pepper). Perhaps the most famous is the peppery Szechwan Duck, steamed and deep-fried and so very tender that even the bones can be eaten.

The Shanghai School is noted for its generous use of soy sauce combined with sugar. Another distinction is the method of chopping the meats and vegetables very, very fine and then sauteeing them together. A delicacy called Lion's Head is one of the most popular Shanghai dishes. It is marinated ground pork rolled into a ball, deep-fried, then cooked with Chinese cabbage.

The fourth distinctive school of Chinese cooking is called Fukien, a coastal area south of Shanghai. Fukien is noted for its soups. All the food is a bit on the sweet side because of a generous use of sugar. The vegetables are cooked soft rather than allowed to remain crisp. Their steamed fish is especially tender and good. Fukien is also famous for its pork and chicken dishes enhanced with a pale red rice wine.

Best known of the five Chinese schools is the Cantonese. Its geographical position near fresh and salt water and its rich agricultural land allowed the Cantonese the widest variety of foodstuffs. Being an international port, Canton reflected the European cuisines which businessmen brought with them.

And, because they were situated near the ocean and major water routes, the Cantonese were travelers and emigrants. They brought their own style of cooking with them, wherever they went, so that both in their homes and in their restaurants overseas, guests became familiar with the dishes of the southern part of China.

The principal method of Cantonese cooking is the quick-fry or toss-fry. Very little oil is used, and this toss-fry method preserves the natural fresh flavor, color and texture of the meat and vegetables, as well as retaining their vitamins. Another characteristic of Cantonese cooking is the crispness of their noodles. They are equally renowned for their version of shark's fin soup.

The ritual of "dim sum" or brunch is peculiar only to the Cantonese. Dim sum are steamed dumplings filled with seafood or meat, or for dessert filled with sweet pastes or preserves. Wealthy businessmen may have dim sum every day, conducting business conferences between courses. On Saturdays and Sundays they bring their families.

However, the Cantonese are not limited to the toss-fry method. They are equally famous for their roasting and grilling. One of the most important dishes is the whole suckling pig. No wedding, feast or New Year's Eve banquet would be complete without serving the pig, colorfully decorated with pineapple and red cherries.

The suckling pig has an added, and to this day, important significance. When a girl marries, the ceremony takes place at the home of the groom's parents where the festivities go on for two days. On the third day the bride, accompanied by her new husband, pays a call on her parents. She brings with her a cold suckling pig sent by the groom's family to indicate that she was a virgin. Her parents proudly call on their close relatives and friends to share the pig.

If she comes home without the pig, she has brought shame to her family and they have lost face; she will never be invited to her parents' home again.

When I began my cooking classes, one of the questions most frequently asked of me was, "How much special equipment will I have to buy to prepare a proper Chinese dinner at home?"

My students invariably registered surprise when I would reply, "Actually, none. I'm sure you have everything you need in your kitchen right now."

However, I knew they wanted to have something typically Chinese to add to the adventure of cooking, so I would suggest that they purchase a wok, a cleaver, a pair of wooden chopsticks and a bamboo-handled copper mesh scoop. Each of these items has unlimited versatility in any kitchen in the world.

The wok, which comes in various sizes, is a concave thin iron pan with a round bottom, and looks like a large salad bowl. The wok has been the main cooking pot in the Chinese kitchen for centuries, and the old fashioned coal, wood or charcoal-burning stoves were designed with round openings in the surface into which the round-bottom woks fit securely. A metal collar was designed later to adapt it to the flat surface of the modern gas and electric stoves. The collar also serves to concentrate the heat into the center of the wok.

For home use I recommend a wok of about a 14-inch diameter, preferably of iron, since stainless steel and aluminum woks heat up too fast and do not distribute the heat evenly. Be sure to buy the collar and a deep lid. Woks are available in the houseware departments of most stores, hardware stores and Chinese food markets.

You can use the wok for every type of Chinese and American cooking. With it you can fry, braise, saute, stew, scramble, simmer, blanch, deep-fry and steam. Indeed, its uses are endless.

But let me repeat, the iron skillet which you already have is almost as effective. It should be about three inches deep and about twelve inches in diameter, with a close-fitting lid.

However, if you do buy a wok, the first thing you must do is to season it. Fill the wok to the brim with hot water and boil for an hour. Pour out the water and dry the wok thoroughly. Wad a paper towel, soak it in vegetable oil, swab the bottom and sides of the wok and heat over a high flame. Remove from the fire, wipe out with clean paper toweling. Now make another swab with oil and continue heating until no more discoloration shows on the clean towel for wiping out. You may have to do this four or five times. Then rinse with warm water and dry thoroughly.

The second most useful utensil in the kitchen is a cleaver, or rather, two cleavers, one larger and heavier than the other. The larger is called a Dai Doh (big knife), and is effective in chopping through bones and shells, in scaling fish, and in pounding or crushing things such as ginger root or garlic. The blade is between 3½ to 3¾ inches wide, and about eight inches long, with a four-inch handle, preferably of wood.

The smaller cleaver is called a Choi Doh, which means vegetable knife. The Choi Doh tapers down to a thinner edge; the blade is five to six inches long, and two to three inches wide with a wooden handle.

Both should be of tempered carbon steel. I stress a wooden handle because it will not conduct

heat and is easier on your hand when you have
a lot of chopping to do. Both look formidable,
but once you get used to them, you will use
nothing else. They are also good for scooping up
scraps of food on the table, saving you the need
for another dish to wash when whatever you
are cutting is to be used immediately.

If you decide to use only one cleaver, buy the
larger Dai Doh.

You are going to need a surface on which to do
all the chopping, pounding, shredding, cutting,
mincing, dicing and thin-slicing with your cleaver.
I am sure that almost every household has a
sizeable breadboard which can serve the purpose.
The Chinese use a round piece of hardwood,
about three to five inches thick, usually a cross-
section of a tree trunk, and generally twelve to
fourteen inches in diameter.

Bamboo chopsticks are so inexpensive that I
suggest you buy them in a package of a dozen at
any Chinese grocery store. Personally, I use
bamboo chopsticks for everything when I cook at
home; for example, to mix the meat with its
marinade, to saute the meat and to dish out the
food from the wok onto the plates.

The dozen-package will last you for years of
cooking and eating. As kitchen utensils they can't
be surpassed—they don't conduct heat, they
don't take any special care, nor do they take up
any room. They can be used in place of an egg
beater, a mixing spoon, wire whisk, cooking fork
or draining spoon.

Although Americans and Europeans prefer the
bamboo chopsticks because they are less slippery
than the ivory or plastic kind, in the olden days
in China the rich families used chopsticks made
of ivory, gold, silver or jade.

When I was about six years old, I had a pair of round-cut jade chopsticks, the top and the bottom two inches of which were heavily plated in gold, and a gold chain at the top held the chopsticks together. Every day when I came to the table for lunch and dinner, I would find the jade chopsticks at my place. Between meals the servant returned them to a drawer in my room.

One day I came to the table and discovered that the servant had forgotten them. A very bad-tempered child, I was upset and showed my displeasure. My sister, a year younger than I, ran into my room and brought out the chopsticks, placing them at my place in a loving gesture. But I was not appeased—angrily I threw them on the floor, where they broke into pieces.

When my grandfather came into the room and saw what I had done, he quietly ordered that bamboo chopsticks be assigned to me from then on. I have always used bamboo chopsticks since; they serve to remind me to control my temper.

The fourth optional utensil is a bamboo-handled copper mesh scoop—indispensable for deep-frying shrimp, noodles, pork and chicken. They come in several sizes, but I would suggest one about six or seven inches in diameter, with a foot-long bamboo handle. I use chopsticks to pick each individual item out of the hot oil, but it will be much easier for you to use the scoop and get them all out at once so that they do not become saturated with the oil or become too browned. The scoop is available in Chinatown, but if you can't find one, you can use the scissors-like metal tongs, or a slotted spoon.

Other American-style utensils you can use are a colander for washing and draining rice and noodles, a sieve, wooden spoon, spatula, standard measuring spoons and cups, and a garlic press, handy to crush ginger root and garlic.

You can use your ordinary two, three and four-quart pots for boiling rice and making soups. A turkey roasting pan is handy for deep-frying sweet and sour fish, Peking Duck or other fowl whose size demands a larger pot.

Steaming fish, fowl, meat and eggs is a popular method of Chinese cooking. Steaming retains the vitamins in the food and is the simplest way to cook anything. It requires no watching other than to be sure that the water doesn't dry out or boil over into the steaming dish.

The steamer looks like a shallow bamboo tray full of holes which allows the steam to penetrate effectively, and the food is placed in heat-proof bowls set in the steamer. Over the steamer goes a deep metal cover to contain the steam generated by the boiling water in the wok base.

The Chinese like to use a big wok as the base in which they place, one on top of the other, as many tiers of bamboo steamers as they have different or greater quantities of food to steam. In this way one can cook three or four different foods at the same time, saving cooking space, time and fuel. For instance, you could prepare an entire dinner of steamed eggplant, chicken with Chinese sausage, steamed fish with black bean sauce and even steamed rice on one burner.

You can buy an aluminum steamer with a deep base, two or three trays with perforated bottoms, and a lid. When you use this type, fill the base with about two to three inches of hot water.

The important thing to remember is that whatever you are steaming should be at least two inches above the boiling water, so that the water does not boil onto the food, and that the steamer must be covered. Do not put the food in the trays until the water is boiling in the base, then turn the heat down, but still maintain the boiling stage.

You can improvise your own steamer in the following ways:

1. Wok. Place a trivet or a metal rack which stands two inches above the water. The food is placed in the bowl in which it will be served. Cover the wok tightly with its own high-domed lid.
2. Dutch oven. Same procedure.
3. Three or four-quart pot. Perforate the bottom of an empty one-pound coffee can. Place it upside down in the pot which has two inches of boiling water. Put the heat-proof bowl of food to be steamed on top of the coffee can, and cover with the pot lid.

There should be enough room between the food and the cover for the steam to circulate.

When removing food from the steamer, be careful not to burn yourself. Take the lid off slowly, let some of the steam escape, and then use hot pads to remove the bowls.

You can use your oven for roasting meat, the stove-top grill for egg foo yung, and the hibachi for many of the appetizer recipes such as barbecued beef or Beef Sadea.

Preparation

The secret to giving a successful dinner party at home, according to all the cookbooks my daughter has consulted since she became a bride, is to select a menu which allows the hostess to enjoy her own party. My ancestors have known this secret for centuries. When you give a Chinese dinner party, approximately 90 per cent of your time will be spent in preparations of the ingredients to be cooked, much of which can be done a day ahead and stored in the freezer or refrigerator.

Before you begin cooking preparations, be sure you have read each recipe through two or three times. Often it will call for certain dried ingredients such as Fun See rice noodles, black mushrooms, a fungus called "Cloud Ear" and a vegetable called "Golden Needle," all of which must be soaked about fifteen minutes before washing, draining and cutting.

Most of the actual cooking by the steaming, roasting, deep-frying and stewing methods can be done in stages several hours before your guests arrive, with the finishing touches taking only a few minutes. Even the quick-frying of vegetables can be done a short while before they are added to the last-minute meat cooking. However, I recommend that novice chefs limit themselves to just one, or at the most two, quick-fry dishes per meal, since quick-frying involves the total readiness of all ingredients, complete concentration, with both hands busy, and rapid cooking over high heat.

Whichever combination of cooking methods you use to prepare a complete dinner, your ingredients may have to be marinated, soaked, chopped, diced, minced, sliced, cubed and/or shredded. This is really the most time-consuming part of the whole cooking procedure. I suggest you do some of it while watching television the night before your party. Remember that everything must be no larger than bite-size because knives are never served at the table.

All the ingredients in each recipe are cut the same size and shape, whether they are vegetables or meat, seafood or fowl. For example, if the recipe calls for thin-slicing, you will thin-slice each ingredient used where possible; if the method is dicing, all should be diced. May I suggest that when you make up your menu, you choose not only different main ingredients and methods of cooking, but different cutting methods as well.

The size and shape of the cutting will depend upon the nature of the food to be cut. If your recipe calls for string beans or bean sprouts with chicken, the natural shape of these two vegetables will dictate that the chicken should be cut in thin strips. If the dish were a combination of chicken and pineapple, the fruit would lend itself to the larger chunk-size or shape, and thus the chicken would be cut chunk-size.

There are three different angles when you slice ingredients: straight, diagonal, and roll-diagonal. Straight slicing is cutting at right angles to the cutting board. You will use this cut for tender, fleshy vegetables such as mushrooms, bamboo shoots, beans and water chestnuts.

Diagonal-slice, which is cutting at a 45° angle, would be used to cut such items as green onions, broccoli, celery and bak choi.

When you are cutting such coarse, fibrous vegetables as carrots, you make a diagonal cut about 1½" from the bottom. For the next 1½" length, roll the carrot half-way around and make the diagonal slice. Keep this up for the length of the vegetable to be cut. What this does is to expose the most surface to the heat and allow the greatest absorption of seasonings and juices.

From largest to smallest, these are the bite-size shapes to cut:

Square	1½" on all sides
Cube	1" on each side
Dice	½" to ⅜" squares
Thin-slice	1½" lengths, 1" widths, ¼"to 1/16" thickness
Shred	Straight slice, then cut into narrow strips 1" to 1½" long, ¼" to ⅛" wide
Chop	Straight cut to the size of a pea
Mince	Chop fine or put through a grinder

Always cut away and discard the gristle and fat from the meat. If you allow the meat to be slightly frozen, it makes it easier to cut. Cut across the grain to get the greatest tenderness out of the meat.

Vegetables must be carefully washed and drained before cutting, since very little water is used in most of the cooking methods. Lettuce and cabbage leaves should be individually washed. All of the ingredients should be as dry as possible in order to prevent splattering when they are added to the hot oil.

Often the main ingredient is marinated for at least 15 minutes, so be sure to allow for that process.

Cooking

When all the advance preparations have been completed, assemble each separate bowl within easy reach of the stove, arranged in the order in which they will be cooked. The cut vegetables should be kept in separate bowls, since they may each take a different cooking time. The tough, fibrous ones such as celery, carrots and cabbage, taking the longest cooking time, will be nearest the stove; the tender leafy vegetables such as spinach, lettuce, bean sprouts, bamboo shoots and water chestnuts behind them, and the very tender vegetables such as Chinese pea pods at the back.

Behind them will be the seasonings and sauces mixed with the thickening agent when the latter is used.

To cut down on cooking time, you may parboil the fibrous vegetables by adding them to boiling water, keeping them in just long enough for the water to regain the boiling stage. Quickly remove them and rinse in cold water to retain their natural color. Drain on paper toweling and set them aside until they are to be used.

Color is a very important part of dinner enjoyment. Green vegetables will not lose their bright color if, during the few minutes of stewing, the lid is not removed.

Now that you have assembled everything you will need, you are ready to cook. This readiness is absolutely essential if you are using the most popular method of Chinese cookery, the quick-fry. Although some cookbooks call this method stir-frying, or toss-fry, and you will find that I often refer to it by its French word, saute, I really prefer to refer to it as quick-fry because it is completely descriptive of the process. It is rapid frying in a preheated pan over high heat and a small amount of oil. Stir-frying and toss-frying will mislead the reader, because you do not toss or stir meat when it is frying or it will become watery. Quick-fry makes for the preservation of the color of the ingredients being fried, such as green vegetables and red meats, and it preserves the vitamin content of the food.

But, no matter what it is called, these three points are unchangeable:

1. The pan is preheated before adding the cooking oil.
2. The cooking oil is preheated before adding the ingredients.
3. The whole process uses the highest heat.

When the wok is preheated and you add the cooking oil, swirl the oil around the bottom and sides before putting in the vegetables or meat. If salt is to be added, it goes in after the meat.

If a clove of garlic or a slice of pared ginger root is called for, it is a good idea to crush the garlic cloves with the heavy handle of your cleaver or a similar heavy object, then peel it before swirling it around the bottom and sides of the fry pan. This releases the juices from the garlic to better permeate the pan. The same is true in the use of the ginger root, which is widely used to add flavor to the oil and to mask the slightly unpleasant odor of shellfish. Both the garlic and the ginger root are kept in the pan until the oil turns them brown, then they are removed and discarded.

When, as it usualy does, the recipe calls for meat and vegetables to be quick-fried, they are cooked separately because the meat (except for pork) takes only a few seconds to fry or it will become tough. The vegetables are fried first, then set aside in a dish until the main ingredient is quick-fried. They are then returned to the pan for the last few seconds of the frying process.

Liquid seasonings such as soy sauce, cooking wine, Hoisin and oyster sauces should be added toward the end because cooking meat in liquid tends to toughen it. And while I think of it, please note that I use the terms light soy sauce and thin soy sauce interchangeably—they're the same. I've done this also with M.S.G. and monosodium glutamate.

Whenever cornstarch is added to the dish, be sure the liquid in the pan, no matter how little there is of it, is at the boiling point. Move the food in the pan away to the sides and make a well in the center, add the cornstarch/water blend with the sauces included, and then quickly mix with the other ingredients.

The last item to be added is usually sesame oil, because its delicate flavor is destroyed when it is heated more than a few seconds.

Wet Steaming   "Jing"

You are undoubtedly familiar with the western method of dry steaming with a solid pan over a bottom boiler full of boiling water. The steam never touches the food.

The Jing wet steaming method consists of cooking food in a pot of wet steam provided by actively boiling water at the bottom. The food is placed on preheated platters or bowls in which it is to be served. There is room around the sides and above the food for the steam to circulate freely without having the water level reach the food.

The delicate taste and texture of fish lends itself especially well to wet steaming. It is the easiest way of all Chinese cooking methods because it does not require watching, other than to be sure that the water does not boil away. Like the quick-fry method, it preserves the flavors and nutrients.

I refer you to the beginning section of this chapter for a detailed description of the Chinese steamer and how you can improvise one.

Remember that the water must be boiling before adding the food to be steamed; then reduce the heat but have it still high enough to maintain the boiling temperature.

Deep-Frying "Jar"

Deep-frying is almost as familiar to the western cook as to the Chinese. Timing and high heat still are essential factors as in the other methods already described.

I recommend any odorless vegetable oil, which can be saved and re-used except when you have deep-fried fish. The oil should be heated to a temperature of about 375° F. If you do not have a thermometer, test for readiness by dropping a small piece of bread into the oil. If the bread sinks and then returns to the surface immediately amidst furious bubbles, it is hot enough.

When you are dipping the food into a batter, let the excess batter drip back into the bowl before dropping into the hot oil. Deep-fry no more than you have room for, so that you can fry all sides evenly. Drain each on paper toweling.

Simmering

This is the same method used by Western cooks, preparing dishes over low heat, and is the method for boiling rice and finishing soup.

Red Cooking "Hung Siu"

Red cooking is a type of stewing with soy sauce so that the food has a reddish-brown color. This is a long, slower process and not as popular as the methods indicated above. It also uses less tender cuts of meat.

Dining Family Style in China

Dining customs differ somewhat in China from those in other countries, so I would like to tell you something about how we usually eat at home in China. In most households the grandparents, the parents and all the children sit together at the same round table three times a day for breakfast, lunch and dinner.

At breakfast time we have the Chinese version of a western-style meal of cereal, ham and eggs, toast and coffee, which is congee, eggs, some dry vegetables and Chinese sausage with tea.

Although we have our main meal at the dinner hour, at luncheon we have at least two or three meat dishes, soup and vegetables, all put on the table at the same time.

In family style, we use the rice bowl first for soup, then rice. We use chopsticks to take the food from the center of the table.

We never serve large pieces of meat. Like everything else, meat is cut into bite-sized pieces before cooking. Everything can be eaten with chopsticks; we never use knives.

After dinner we always have some fresh fruit to take away the heavy taste and clear the mouth and throat.

Many people ask me, "Why is it that most Chinese people never have a weight problem?" It may be because we eat very little pastry, bread or cake.

The world's reaction to President Nixon's historic trip to Peking I will leave for others to interpret. However, you might be interested in my personal reaction, which I think is shared by every person of Chinese origin. I am pleased that journalists from the Western world were impressed by the excellence of Chinese cuisine, but at the same time I am confused and just a little indignant over the "discovery" that the Chinese are excellent chefs. The visiting journalists in print and television commentators in person were ecstatic over their first-time experiences in dining on such delicacies as Shark's Fin Soup, Bird's Nest Soup, Sweet & Sour Fish, and Peking Duck.

They need not have gone to China to enjoy these dishes, for they have been served over many decades in Chinese restaurants outside Taiwan, Hong Kong and mainland China.

I have had the delightful opportunity to educate hundreds of people in the pleasures of Chinese cuisine over the past twelve years, so that many who came into my restaurant to order only the things they were familiar with—chop suey, chow mein and Egg Foo Yung—have since learned to broaden their taste treats.

And just as this cookbook has been written to make it possible to share my recipes with wider audiences, I think it will expand your opportunities to enjoy Chinese dishes both at home and when you dine out if I set down a few suggestions, some of which apply to any dining-out experience.

It is obvious that the best and most authentic Chinese food is only to be found in a restaurant operated and staffed by Chinese. The procedures I am about to suggest can be followed in the small establishment where the owner is the cook and there is but one waiter (and the larger restaurants with a complete staff).

My first suggestion is that you order a la carte instead of the suggested "Family Dinner." As you know, a la carte means that the dishes are cooked to order rather than prepared ahead of time and left warm in the steam tables. When you see "Soup du Jour" or its English translation, "Soup of the Day," on a menu, you can be 99 percent certain that it has been made ahead of time and is being kept heated in the steam table. There is nothing wrong with this method, except that if you have a gourmet's palate, you undoubtedly like your soup to be made to order so that its delicate seasoning has not been dissipated by time and steam.

Virtually every Chinese restaurant is capable of serving excellent soup and fried rice; they are basic to all Chinese cooking. But unless you order them a la carte, the soup is ladled out of the steam table, and so is the fried rice. Since these two dishes are usually included in "Family Dinners," they must be prepared in advance, because they take fifteen to twenty minutes to cook to order.

I recommend ordering Wor Won Ton Soup, which must be made to order since chicken, shrimp, black mushrooms, abalone, water chestnuts, pea pods and bamboo shoots are added to the basic soup recipe.

As for the fried rice, I would suggest that you order subgum fried rice, because the cooked rice is freshly fried and the flavor piqued with chicken, peas, mushrooms, onions and eggs.

Perhaps I should say here that the Chinese eat white rice only with their meals in order to enjoy more fully the nuances of the main dishes. This is comparable to an American-style dinner with rolls which are served plain rather than accompanied by peanut butter, jam or jelly.

In order for you to get the most out of your dining experiences, it might be wise to remind you of our philosophy about eating. The Chinese like to enjoy many different textures, flavors and colors during every meal. We prefer something crisp to the teeth, like bamboo shoots, crunchy like cashews and almonds, sweet and sour tastes like almond duck, and velvet-like black mushrooms, besides enjoying the varied tastes of pork, chicken, beef, seafood—I could go on and on. But in order to enjoy these variations, we must limit the amount we eat of each.

Now, in ordering a la carte (or planning your own home dinner menu), there is a simple system to follow. The total number of main dishes should equal the number of people in your party, or one order per person. One order divided up gives a small but adequate serving to each of four persons.

Let's say there are four people in your party, and your guests would enjoy seafood, fowl, beef and perhaps a sweet and sour fish, plus vegetables. You might ask your captain or waiter to recommend four dishes in these categories.

While he is naming the dishes, have him point to them in your menu. There is usually a description of each entree, in case his English is faulty. Note the price printed beside each dish; mentally add up the four prices and you have the approximate cost of your dinner, since there is usually no charge for the white rice, pots of tea and dessert cookies which almost always accompany a meal.

If I were your waiter or captain, I might suggest for the four of you an order each of Mo Goo Gai Peen (chicken), Sizzling Go Ba (shrimp with meat, chicken and pea pods), Wu's Beef (sauteed marinated beef strips), and Sweet and Sour Pork.

If there are five of you, I would suggest the same four main dishes, but increase the quantities. You will note that they add up to five orders, which is the same number as your party.

1	order Mo Goo Gai Peen
1½	orders Sizzling Go Ba
1½	orders Wu's Beef
1	order Sweet and Sour Pork
5	orders

For six people, the order might be:

1½	orders Mo Goo Gai Peen
1½	orders Sizzling Go Ba
2	orders Wu's Beef
1	order Sweet and Sour Pork
6	orders

For eight people, either increase the quantities, or perhaps add two orders of Lobster Cantonese.

The important point to remember is that you will need a minimum order of one main dish per person, just as in an American restaurant you order one meal for each person in the party; you would not ask for only a half-order of prime rib.

This formula holds true for the "Family Dinner" which you find on most Chinese restaurant menus. It is based on a minimum of two people and usually indicates two main dishes. For every additional person over the minimum, an extra dish is added. For instance, it might read, "For three persons add Almond Duck. For four persons add Almond Duck and Lobster Cantonese." Add the number of main dishes and you will see that it equals the number of persons to be served.

All of which reminds me of a story. One of my customers had just lunched with Bob Hope, and he called my secretary to tell her this joke. Someone asked Mr. Hope, "Why did President Nixon take Henry Kissinger and Secretary Rogers to Peking with him?" and Hope replied, "Because with three you get egg roll!"

Appetizers

Fried Shrimp
🔄 Wo Dib Har 🔄

HAVE READY:
   16 shrimp, size 16/20 (about 1 pound)

STEP 1:
   Shell, devein and butterfly-cut the shrimp and put them in the refrigerator overnight. If you are serving them the same day, be sure to dry them thoroughly on paper toweling after washing.

HAVE READY:

1 cup all-purpose flour	1 teaspoon salt
¼ cup cornstarch	1 teaspoon vegetable oil
1 teaspoon baking powder	1 egg
	1 cup water

STEP 2:
   Mix the above ingredients until they make a smooth batter of the consistency of a thin ribbon of liquid·

HAVE READY:
   1 quart vegetable oil

STEP 3:
   Heat 1 quart vegetable oil in a deep fryer until it is hot (375° F.). Dip each shrimp into the batter, letting the excess drip back into the bowl. Slip the shrimp into the hot oil, let fry until golden brown on both sides for 1 or 2 minutes. Fry only 2 or 3 at a time. Remove and drain on paper toweling.

Fried Wonton with Sweet & Sour Sauce
🔄 Jar Won Ton 🔄

HAVE READY:
  2 dozen wonton wrappers
  1 quart vegetable oil

STEP 1:
  Cut each wonton square in half, then put halves together. Cut a 1-inch slit in the center and pull one end through the slit.

STEP 2:
  Heat the oil in a deep kettle until it is very hot (375° F.). Drop the wontons into the oil and fry for 1 minute, browning on both sides. Remove and drain on paper toweling. Makes 24 wontons.

SWEET & SOUR SAUCE

HAVE READY:
  1 cup catsup
  ¼ cup vinegar
  3 tablespoons sugar
  1 tablespoon cornstarch blended
      with 3 tablespoons water
  3 drops red food coloring (optional)

METHOD:
  Combine the catsup, vinegar and sugar in a pot and bring to a boil. When boiling, add the cornstarch blend and bring again to a boil, stirring into a smooth syrup. Remove from fire and pour into a bowl for serving. If you like a brighter red color in the sauce, stir in food coloring before serving.

  Serve the crisp, hot wontons with the sweet and sour sauce for dipping.

Crab Puffs
⁂ Jar Hai Hop ⁂

HAVE READY:

1 cup cooked crab meat (not canned)	⅓ cup cream cheese
¼ teaspoon salt	1 egg white
1 pinch white pepper	20 square wonton wrappers
1 quart vegetable oil	

MAKE PASTE:

Add the salt and pepper to the crabmeat and mix well. Then add the cream cheese and mix thoroughly until it is very smooth.

STUFF PUFF:

With a pastry brush, wet the four edges of the square wonton wrapper with egg white. Put about ½ tablespoon of crab mixture in the center of the square and bring edges together to form a triangle, carefully sealing the edges. Then take two angles of the triangle and bring them up to the third angle, after brushing the edges with egg white for a sealer. Appetizers are now ready to be deep-fried, or stored in the freezer for later use.

DEEP-FRY:

Heat 1 quart of vegetable oil in a deep kettle until it is very hot (375° F.). Submerge the puffs and turn them over until they are uniformly browned (about 2 minutes). Remove and drain on paper toweling.

Serve immediately.

Makes 20 puffs.

Barbecued Pork
🔁 Char Siu 🔁

HAVE READY:

1 1-pound pork tender-
loin, cut in two strips
¼ cup dark Chinese
soy sauce
1 teaspoon light Chinese
soy sauce
3 tablespoons catsup
1 teaspoon sugar
3 tablespoons Hoisin
sauce
2 cloves garlic, crushed
1 tablespoon red wine

STEP 1:

Make a marinade of the soy sauces, catsup, sugar,
Hoisin sauce, garlic and red wine and marinate
the pork overnight, or for a minimum of 4 hours.

STEP 2:

Preheat oven to 350° F. Place marinated pork
strips on oven rack, with pan underneath to
catch the drippings. After 20 minutes, lower the
heat to 300° F. and brush both sides with the
marinade and barbecue 20 minutes. Brush both
sides again, turn over and barbecue 15 more
minutes. Brush, turn over, and complete barbecu-
ing after 15 minutes.

STEP 3:

Remove from the oven. If the pork is to be served
as an appetizer, cut into thin strips. If main
course, cut into larger pieces.

Serves four.

Paper Wrapped Chicken
⚛ Gee Bau Gai ⚛

MARINATE ONE HOUR:
- 1 cup uncooked, boned chicken, light or
  dark meat, sliced thin
- 1 tablespoon Hoisin sauce
- 1 tablespoon dark Chinese soy sauce
- 1/4 teaspoon light Chinese soy sauce
- 1/4 teaspoon sugar (optional)
- 1/4 teaspoon sesame oil (optional)

HAVE READY:
- 2 quarts vegetable oil
- 8 4-inch squares of aluminum foil or rice paper
  (foil is easier to use, but be sure there are no
  holes in either the foil or the paper

STEP 1:

Heat the vegetable oil in a large kettle until it
is hot (375° F.).

STEP 2:

Meanwhile, in the center of each square place
4 pieces of the marinated chicken. Fold over into
a triangular shape, then turn over each flap twice.
Tuck in the two ends. It is very important that
the chicken is sealed in carefully or the wrapper
will open and spill out the contents during deep-
frying. When oil is hot, slip in the foil triangles
and deep-fry for 3 minutes. When they puff up
and come to the surface, they are done.

Makes eight. Serve as appetizers while hot.

Egg Roll
⇄ Gai Dahn Quen ⇄

HAVE READY:

7 eggs	¼ cup baby shrimp
1 quart vegetable oil	½ cup thin-sliced
½ cup chopped white	water chestnuts
boiled chicken meat	1¼ teaspoon salt
½ cup thin-sliced	½ teaspoon white
bamboo shoots	pepper
½ cup thin-sliced celery	¼ teaspoon M.S.G.
heart	(optional)

STEP 1:

Beat 6 eggs. Preheat 6-inch frying pan over medium fire, then swirl around 1 teaspoon vegetable oil. Put one-fourth of the eggs in at each time until you make four skins, then set aside and let cool in the refrigerator.

STEP 2:

Preheat the wok, then pour in 2 tablespoons oil, brushing bottom and sides. Quick-fry the chicken for a few seconds, then add the bamboo shoots, celery heart, baby shrimp, water chestnuts, salt, pepper and M.S.G., stirring for 2 minutes. Drain out liquid and refrigerate ingredients until cold.

STEP 3:

Beat 1 egg in a small dish and brush over skins. Spoon on the filling (Step 2), roll very tight, and seal ends with egg. Now deep-fry in vegetable oil at 350° F. for 2 minutes, until they rise to the surface.

To serve, cut into 2-inch pieces.

Serves four.

Chicken Sticks
🔁 Teem Suen Gai Yik 🔁

HAVE READY:
   8 broiler chicken wings
      salt

Separate the chicken wings into 3 pieces at the joints. Discard the wing tips. On the remaining 2 sections, with a sharp knife loosen the meat from the joint and pull down to the end of the bone and over the bottom of the bone to form a ball. It will look like a umbrella that is turned inside-out, or a candied apple on a stick. Salt the balls.

MAKE BATTER:
   1 cup all-purpose flour
   ½ cup cornstarch
   1 teaspoon baking powder
   ½ teaspoon salt
   1½ cups water
   1 teaspoon vegetable oil

Mix these ingredients in a bowl until you have a smooth batter.

HAVE READY:
   1 quart vegetable oil

METHOD:
Heat the oil in a kettle until it is very hot (375° F.). Dip the chicken balls into the batter, allowing the excess to drain off. Drop each into the hot oil and deep-fry for 7 to 10 minutes, depending upon the size of the balls. Place on platter and serve with a sweet and sour dip. (see page 27 for sweet and sour sauce recipe)

Makes 16 chicken sticks.

Beef Sadea
🔄 Sadea Ngau Yoke 🔄

PREPARE THE NIGHT BEFORE:
1-pound flank steak from which gristle and fat is removed. Cut about 1½ inches from one end, and about 1 inch from the other. Trim the long sides. You will be left with the mid-section of the flank steak. Store it in the freezer overnight so that it will cut more easily. Also, obtain **16 6-inch barbecue bamboo skewers.**

PREPARE MARINADE:
1 teaspoon Indian curry powder
2 tablespoons dark Chinese soy sauce
1 teaspoon light Chinese soy sauce
1 teaspoon red cooking wine
1 teaspoon sugar

STEP 1:
Cut across the grain of frozen steak into 32 strips 1/16 of an inch thick. Lace two strips like peppermint ribbon candy on a skewer, one following the other.

STEP 2:
Pour the marinade in a shallow pan. Roll the skewered beef in the marinade and place each skewer on a platter with the skewer over the side. Pour the remaining marinade over the beef, and marinate for 3 or 4 hours.

STEP 3:
When ready to cook, lightly grease your stove-top grill (or skillet) and preheat. Before placing each beef skewer on the grill, let the excess marinade drip back onto the platter. Grill just long enough to brown both sides of the skewered meat. When ready to serve, bring individual miniature preheated hibachis (either with charcoal or sterno) and allow guests to barbecue their beef to their own tastes.

Makes 16 skewers.

Barbecued Beef
🔁 Siu Ngau Yoke 🔁

HAVE READY:

½ pound top sirloin, cut into 16 bite-size pieces

1 tablespoon dark Chinese soy sauce

1 teaspoon light Chinese soy sauce

1 ½" slice fresh ginger root

2 cloves crushed garlic (optional)

1 teaspoon red cooking wine

½ teaspoon sugar

METHOD:

Prepare a marinade of the soy sauces, ginger root, garlic, wine and sugar, and marinate the sirloin pieces overnight, then broil in an oven for 3 minutes on each side. Serve with colored toothpicks as hors d'oeuvres.

Allows 4 pieces per person when serving four.

I never tire of watching Robert Redford and his two children when they visit my restaurant. They always order Beef Sadea and seem to enjoy the process of cooking, each with his own hibachi, as much as they do the actual eating.

It is because making Beef Sadea is like a mini-barbecue that it is such a delightful family or party dish. Adults and children all seem to enjoy the do-it-yourself cooking . . . as long as they don't have to worry about the dirty dishes!

Rumaki
🔁 Jar Gai Kon Inn Yoke 🔁

HAVE READY:

1 star anise
1 green onion with stem
1 teaspoon dark
   Chinese soy sauce
½ teaspoon light
   Chinese soy sauce

½ teaspoon salt
2 cups water
½ pound chicken livers
1 small can whole
   water chestnuts
8 slices of thin bacon

PREPARE LIVERS:

Put the star anise, green onion with stem tied in a knot, the soy sauces and salt, with 2 cups of water, in a kettle and bring to a boil. Boil for 1 minute, add the chicken livers, boil 5 minutes more.

Drain the livers and set aside in the refrigerator until thoroughly cold before cutting them.

PREPARE BACON AND CHESTNUTS:

While the livers are chilling, slice the water chestnuts into 2 pieces, and cut the 8 bacon slices in half. Remove the muscle and vein from the chilled livers and cut into chunks about ½ by 1 inch in size. Place 1 slice of water chestnut on one end of the bacon half, next to the flat surface of the liver slice for ease in rolling. Roll tightly and secure with a wooden toothpick through the bacon, chestnut and liver. They are now ready for cooking.

(To save time, you can make these appetizers in advance and store them in your freezer until you want to cook them. However, allow them to defrost before deep-frying to avoid having the hot oil splatter from the congealed moisture.)

COOK RUMAKI:

There are three ways: broiling, baking or deep-frying. I prefer deep-frying. If you wish to bake or broil, use a low rack on a cookie sheet so that the bacon fat can drip away. When the bacon is crisp, remove and drain on paper toweling, and serve while hot.

To deep-fry, heat a quart of vegetable oil until it is hot (375° F.). Fry the rumaki for 10 minutes or until the bacon is crisp.

Barbecued Spare Ribs
🌀 Siu Pai Kwat 🌀

HAVE READY:

1 12-rib slab of pork spare ribs which have been cracked down the center for easy separation after they have been cooked. Cut off skin and fat.	1 teaspoon light Chinese soy sauce
	3 tablespoons Hoisin sauce
	2 tablespoons catsup
	2 cloves garlic chopped fine
2 tablespoons dark Chinese soy sauce	2 tablespoons sugar (optional)

STEP 1:

Prepare a marinade of the soy sauces, catsup, Hoisin sauce, garlic and sugar, and brush over the spare ribs with a pastry brush. Turn over, brush again. Place ribs on a platter, cover with foil and marinate overnight in the refrigerator.

STEP 2:

To cook, transfer the marinated spare ribs to a shallow pan. Preheat the oven to 400° F. and bake the ribs for 20 minutes. Reduce the heat to 350° F. and bake for an additional 30 minutes.

STEP 3:

Remove from the oven to a cutting board. Separate into two slabs along the center crack, then cut into individual bite-size pieces.

Serve hot immediately.

Serves four.

Shrimp Toast
🌀 Har Dor See 🌀

HAVE READY:

½ pound uncooked shrimp

¼ teaspoon sesame oil (optional)

¼ teaspoon light Chinese soy sauce

1 pinch white pepper

1 pinch salt

8 slices two-day old white bread, sliced very thin. If you have no old bread, put fresh bread in the refrigerator overnight before using.

1 quart vegetable oil

PREPARE SHRIMP PASTE:

Clean and devein shrimp, and put through a meat grinder. Add sesame oil, soy sauce, pepper and salt, and mix well.

CUT BREAD ROUNDS:

Use small circle cutter (½ to 1 inch in diameter) and cut 32 rounds from the bread slices—about four pieces per slice.

ASSEMBLE SANDWICHES

Spread the shrimp paste evenly on the 16 rounds of bread, keeping the filling within the outer edges of the circle. Top each circle with a bread circle and press edges together gently, to keep the filling from coming out during the deep-frying.

(At this point, you can store the shrimp toast rounds in the freezer until you want to deep-fry them.)

DEEP-FRY:

Heat 1 quart vegetable oil in a deep kettle until it is hot (375° F.). Drop each round into the oil, turning to brown on each side, and fry for 1 or 2 minutes. If you deep-fry longer, the toast will absorb the oil and become greasy. Remove and drain on paper toweling. Serve immediately, while hot.

Makes 16 toast rounds.

Diamond Shrimp Balls
卍 Jar Har Kow 卍

MIX INTO A SMOOTH PASTE:

1 pound uncooked shrimp, cleaned, deveined, ground or chopped fine (about 1½ cups)
1 teaspoon vegetable oil
1 teaspoon red cooking wine
½ teaspoon salt
1 teaspoon light Chinese soy sauce
2 teaspoons cornstarch
⅓ egg, beaten slightly
1 pinch M.S.G. (optional)
1 pinch white pepper

HAVE READY:

6 slices day-old white bread or chill fresh bread in the freezer to make it easier to cut. Dice into cubes like croutons.

HEAT:

1 quart vegetable oil in a kettle to 375° F.

STEP 1:

Put a little oil on your hands. Roll the shrimp paste into balls. Then put the croutons in a flat dish and roll the balls over the croutons (one at a time) so that they will adhere to every part of the balls.

STEP 2:

Drop the balls into the hot oil, but not too many at one time because they will jar each other and flatten the diamond-like facets of the croutons. Deep-fry about 3 minutes, turning them occasionally so that they will be a uniform golden brown. Remove, drain on paper toweling and serve hot.

Makes about 16 balls.

Bamboo Shrimp Roll
🔁 Juk Suhn Har Quen 🔁

MIX INTO A SMOOTH PASTE:

½ pound uncooked shrimp, cleaned, deveined, ground or chopped fine (16/20 size shrimp makes about ¾ cup ground shrimp)

1 teaspoon vegetable oil

½ teaspoon red cooking wine

1 teaspoon light Chinese soy sauce

¼ teaspoon salt

3 teaspoons cornstarch

½ egg slightly beaten

dash pepper

dash M.S.G. (optional)

HAVE READY:

16 strips Shanghai Spring Roll Dough, cut into 2" by 3" strips. If Spring Roll Dough is unavailable, substitute wonton wrappers.

32 strips of bamboo shoots (canned) cut into ½" by 2½" slices.

White of egg

STEP 1:

Place 1 teaspoon of shrimp paste on the 2" by 3" strip of dough, leaving ¼" margin on three sides, and leaving ¾" margin on the far end. Place 2 strips of the bamboo shoots crosswise on the dough strip, so that the ends extend ¼" on each side. Roll up the dough strip until within ¾" of end, then dip the back of a spoon in the eggwhite and brush across dough end to serve as an adhesive. Finish rolling strips and place on a plate to be ready for deep-frying.

STEP 2:

Heat 1 quart vegetable oil in a deep fryer until the oily is very hot (375° F.). Gently drop in shrimp rolls and deep-fry for about 3 minutes, or until golden brown. Remove and drain on paper toweling.

Serve immediately. Makes 16 rolls.

Soups

Quick Winter Melon Soup
🔁 Dung Kwa Tong 🔁

HAVE READY:
- 1 pound winter melon (buy by the pound)
- 2 cans chicken broth
- 1 can water
- 1 cup diced boned uncooked chicken
- 1 cup sliced canned water chestnuts
- ½ cup canned sliced mushrooms

STEP 1:

Scrape away seeds and pulp from the melon piece, pare rind and cut fleshy portion into cubes.

STEP 2:

Combine chicken broth and water in a pot and bring to a boil. Add the chicken and cook uncovered over high heat for 5 minutes.

STEP 3:

Add the winter melon cubes, water chestnuts and mushrooms and cook partially covered, over medium heat, for 15 minutes.

Serves four.

Wor Wonton Soup
🔁 Won Ton Woh 🔁

MIX IN A BOWL:
- ¾ cup ground lean pork
- 4 uncooked shrimp, peeled, deveined and chopped fine
- 2 tablespoons chopped canned water chestnuts
- ½ teaspoon cornstarch
- ¼ teaspoon salt
- ¼ teaspoon cooking sherry
- ¼ teaspoon dark Chinese soy sauce

HAVE READY:
   16 wonton circle wrappers
   1 egg white

PREPARE WONTONS:
   To assemble wontons, place ¼ teaspoon of pork and shrimp mixture into the center of each wrapper. Dip a finger into the egg white, then moisten the edges of the circle. Fold into half, sealing edges. Then bring the outside edges together, sealing with egg white. Turn down so that it resembles a hat with a brim. It is important that the edges are securely sealed so that the meat does not come out when the wontons are immersed in hot water.

   To boil wontons, bring 2 quarts of water to boil in a large kettle. When it reaches a rolling boil, add the wontons, cover and cook over a high heat for 10 minutes. Then reduce to medium heat and boil for 20 minutes more. Drain in colander and under cold water rinse well.

HAVE READY:

2 cans chicken broth (skim off fat)	½ cup sliced canned water chestnuts
2 cans water	½ cup sliced canned bamboo shoots
½ cup medium-sized black mushrooms (measured after washing and soaking for 20 minutes in hot water)	½ cup cleaned, deveined shrimp halves
	1 cup pea pods
½ cup white or dark boned chicken meat sliced into 2″ strips	½ cup barbecued pork, sliced (see recipe for barbecued pork)
	1 teaspoon salt
	¼ teaspoon sesame oil

PREPARE SOUP:
   Bring broth and water to boil in a large kettle, over high heat. Add the black mushrooms and chicken, cover and cook over high heat for 5 minutes. Now add the wontons, cover, bring again to a boil and cook for 5 minutes. Skim off froth.

Add water chestnuts and bamboo shoots, return to a boil, add the shrimp and pea pods, and again return to a boil. Finally add the barbecued pork, salt and sesame oil, and serve immediately.

Serves four, generously.

Fun See Soup
🔄 Fun See Tong 🔄

HAVE READY:

1 cup rice vermicelli (Chinese "fun see")	1 teaspoon cornstarch blended with 2 teaspoons water
1 can water	3 lightly beaten egg whites
2 cans chicken broth (skim off fat)	
1 cup thin-sliced uncooked white chicken meat	¼ cup finely diced cooked Virginia ham
1 teaspoon salt	½ teaspoon sesame oil

STEP 1:

Soak rice vermicelli in cold water for 15 minutes. Drain off water, and cut into 3" strips.

STEP 2:

Bring to boil in a 2-quart kettle, the can of water and the 2 cans of chicken broth.

STEP 3:

In a bowl, mix the chicken meat with the salt and the cornstarch blend. When soup is boiling, stir it in, being careful to separate the chicken meat so that it will not stick together. Cover and bring to a boil, then add the vermicelli and egg whites, stir for several minutes, and take off heat.

STEP 4:

Pour immediately into a soup tureen, add the sesame oil and sprinkle the ham over the top as a garnish. Serve hot.

Serves four.

Sizzling Rice Soup
🔃 Go Ba Tong 🔃

PREPARE THE DAY BEFORE:

Boil **1 pound of white rice** slowly, covered, for 1 hour. Let cool and scoop out all loose grains, leaving the bottom layer. Now scrape out the layer in sections and keep overnight until the pieces solidify.

HAVE READY:

- 2 cans chicken broth
- 1 can hot water
- ¼ cup Chinese cabbage
- ¼ cup black mushrooms, soaked overnight and thin-sliced (if not available, use sliced canned mushrooms)
- ¼ cup pea pods
- ¼ cup bamboo shoots, thin-sliced
- ¼ cup barbecued pork, cut into 1" squares (or thin-sliced chicken or Virginia ham)
- ¼ cup small shrimp
- 2 quarts vegetable oil
- ¼ teaspoon sesame oil
- 1 tablespoon chopped green onion

STEP 1:

Bring the broth and water to a boil, then put in the cabbage. Now add the mushrooms, pea pods and bamboo shoots, and when it comes to a boil again, add the pork and shrimp, and turn off the heat.

STEP 2:

Deep-fry the rice sections (go ba) in the vegetable oil, testing for readiness by dropping in a tiny piece. If it pops up instantly, the oil is hot enough. Ladle the rice into the soup, and just before serving, add the sesame oil and green onion.

Serves four.

Abalone Soup

⚛ Bao Yue Tong ⚛

HAVE READY:
- 2 cans chicken broth (skim off fat)
- 1 can water
- ½ cup cooked white meat of chicken, sliced
- 1 8-ounce can of abalone, drained (but reserve liquid)
- 1 green onion with stem, chopped
- 1 teaspoon dry sherry

METHOD:

Bring the broth and water to a boil. Add the reserved liquid from the abalone can, and return to a boil. Add the chicken and abalone, stir and immediately turn off the heat. It is important not to overcook the abalone or it will become rubbery. Add the onion and wine, and serve.

Serves four.

Egg Drop Soup

⚛ Dahn Far Tong ⚛

HAVE READY:
- 2 cans chicken broth with fat skimmed off
- 1 can water
- 2 tablespoons cornstarch blended with 4 tablespoons water
- 2 eggs, beaten slightly
- 1 tablespoon chopped scallions

METHOD:

Heat soup and water, covered, until boiling. Add the cornstarch blend, then turn off heat. Now add the eggs, pouring them in a light stream, stirring lightly. Add scallions and serve immediately.

Serves four.

46

Chicken Cream of Corn Soup
🀰 Gai Yik Suk Mai Tong 🀰

HAVE READY:
- 1 can (1 pound 1 ounce) cream style golden sweet corn
- 1 can chicken broth (skim off fat)
- ½ can water
- 1 tablespoon cornstarch blended with 3 tablespoons water
- 2 eggs, lightly beaten with a fork

METHOD:
Bring the corn, broth and water to a rolling boil. Add the cornstarch blend and mix in thoroughly. Turn off heat. Pour the eggs in a thin stream, stirring constantly. Serve hot.

Serves four.

Chicken Asparagus Soup
🀰 Lu Suhn Gai Tong 🀰

HAVE READY:
- 2 small cans asparagus (preferably yellow— drain and reserve the liquid)
- 1 can chicken broth with fat skimmed off
- ½ can water
- ¼ cup finely-chopped Virginia ham (boiled ham is a substitute)

METHOD:
Bring the broth, water and the asparagus liquid to a boil. Add the asparagus stalks and return to a boil. Turn off heat and garnish with the chopped ham. Serve immediately.

Serves four.

Chinese Greens & Bean Curd Soup
🌀 Ching Choy Dow Fu Tong 🌀

HAVE READY:
- 1 can chicken broth with fat skimmed off
- 1 can water
- 1½ cups of heart of Chinese cabbage, cut into 1" pieces
- 1 square fresh bean curd (3" x 3" x 1") cut into 1" squares
- ¼ cup Chinese pea pods

METHOD:
Bring the water and broth to a boil. When boiling, add cabbage and bean curd. Return to a boil and cook uncovered for 3 to 4 minutes, or until the cabbage is tender. Add the pea pods, take off flame immediately and serve.

Serves four.

Hot & Sour Soup
🌀 Suen Lat Tong 🌀

HAVE READY:
- 2 cans chicken broth
- 1 can water
- 1 cup cooked, unboned, thin-sliced chicken
- 1 cup presoaked Chinese black mushrooms, cut into strips
- 1 cup bamboo shoots, cut into strips
- 1 cup canned sliced Chinese mustard pickles (be sure to wash off the pickling hot sauce)
- ¾ cup bean curd cut into strips
- 2 eggs
- ¼ teaspoon sesame oil
- ¼ teaspoon pepper

STEP 1:
Bring the chicken broth and water to a boil over high heat, covered, and skim off the fat. While the broth is boiling, add the chicken, cook

5 minutes, then add the mushrooms, bamboo shoots, mustard pickles and bean curds, and continue to cook covered over high heat for 10 minutes more.

STEP 2:
In a small bowl, mix:

   2 tablespoons white vinegar
   1 tablespoon light Chinese soy sauce
   2 tablespoons dark Chinese soy sauce
   ¼ teaspoon salt
   1½ teaspoons Chinese hot sauce (not Tabasco sauce)
   1 tablespoon cornstarch

STEP 3:
Mix and add this sauce to the broth, cook for 3 minutes.

Stir together 2 slightly beaten eggs, ¼ teaspoon sesame oil and ¼ teaspoon pepper, and add to the soup. Serve immediately.

Serves four.

Home-made Chicken Broth
🔃 Kar Sheun Gai Tong 🔃

(We use canned chicken broth as a main ingredient for cooking because it saves time and the taste is the same as the homemade broth. However, we do have a respect for homemade chicken broth.)

HAVE READY:
   1 4-pound stewing chicken
   5 quarts water

STEP 1:
Clean the chicken, removing the yellow fat pockets from either side of the tail. Salt the inside.

STEP 2:

Bring the water to a boil, then immerse the chicken. Cover and return to a boil. To insure that the water does not boil over, place two wooden chopsticks across the top of the kettle, then set the cover on them.

Reduce the heat to a simmer and cook the chicken for 4 hours, occasionally skimming off fat and residue.

STEP 3:

Now let it cool, and discard the skin and bones. You can save the chicken meat easily for recipes that call for chicken. Pour into a glass jar, cover tightly and store in the refrigerator. It will last for two to three weeks if once a week you bring it to a boil, chill and return to the refrigerator.

For clear broth, strain before using.

When Danny Kaye invited me to his house to show me his Chinese kitchen, I looked into his refrigerator and saw a covered jar of stock. He explained that whenever his career took him out of town, he would call his house once a week to remind his Chinese housekeeper to boil the stock. I knew then that Danny was an accomplished Chinese cook!

Sam See Soup

Sam See Tong

HAVE READY:

2 cans chicken broth
1 can water
1 ¼" slice fresh ginger root
1 cup lean pork, cut into thin strips
1 cup white chicken meat, cut into thin strips
1 cup Chinese black mushrooms, cut into thin strips (should be soaked overnight)
1 cup canned bamboo shoots, cut into thin strips
1 cup pea pods, cut into thin lengthwise strips
¼ teaspoon salt
½ can abalone, cut into thin strips

STEP 1:
Into a large kettle, pour the broth and water. Cover, bring to a boil over high heat, and skim off fat. As it boils, add the ginger and pork, cover and cook another 5 minutes. Then add the chicken, cover, and cook 5 minutes.

STEP 2:
Now add the mushrooms and bamboo shoots; cover and cook to the boiling point, skimming off the top to keep the soup clear. Add pea pods and salt, and cook for a few seconds.

STEP 3:
Turn off the heat, add the abalone, remove the piece of ginger, and serve immediately.

Serves four.

Whole Winter Melon Soup
↻ Dun Dung Kwa Chung ↻

PREPARE MELON:
Select a winter melon about 10" high, wash and slice off the lid about 3" from the stem. Scoop out seeds and pulp in the center section, then make "tiger teeth" notches about ¾" deep around the rim of the melon. Pare off outer skin from the teeth, cut the fleshy part in small pieces and use in the soup. Place the melon in an oven-proof bowl and set aside.

PREPARE SOUP:

1 can chicken broth	¼ cup diced Virginia ham
2 cans water	
1 cup diced white un-cooked chicken meat	¼ cup canned bamboo shoots, diced
¼ cup canned lotus seeds	¼ cup canned abalone, diced

Put all the above ingredients except the abalone in the melon.

51

STEAM MELON:

Pour about 3 inches of boiling water into the bottom of a deep kettle. If you have a rack with lift-out handles, use it and put the bowl with the winter melon on it. If not, a simple Chinese method is to place a kitchen towel in the bottom of the kettle, place the bowl on it and bring up the four corners over the melon. When this is done, you merely lift out the melon/bowl by the four corners of the towel. Cover and steam over medium heat for 2 hours; after 1 hour check to see if the water level is still at 3 inches, and if not, add boiling water. When the melon is done, the white meat on its lining will be translucent.

Just before serving, add the abalone and steam for 1 minute.

When you serve the soup, scoop the flesh carefully from the sides of the wall but not too deeply, especially from the bottom, or the soup will spill out.

Serves four to six.

Shark's Fin Soup
🔁 Yue Chi Tong 🔁

HAVE READY:

4 ounces dried shark's fin	2 teaspoons cornstarch blended with 2 tablespoons water
1 ½" slice ginger root	¾ teaspoon salt
3 quarts water	1 teaspoon light soy sauce
3 cans chicken broth	1 teaspoon brandy or wine
½ cup finely cut chicken breast	
¼ cup finely cut Virginia ham	

STEP 1:

Soak shark's fin overnight in cold water, then boil over medium heat with the ginger root for 3 hours. Drain and discard the ginger root.

STEP 2:

Put the shark's fin and chicken broth into a soup pot with 3 cans water, then boil over a slow fire for another 2 hours. Now add the chicken and ham, and boil for 10 minutes, then put in the cornstarch blend and boil for 2 more minutes. Just before serving, put in the salt, soy sauce, brandy or wine.

Serves four.

(Note: If you wish a different taste, mash 2 salted hardboiled egg yolks and stir into the soup. The egg yolks also add color.)

Jack Benny was a frequent diner at my restaurant, and each time I greeted him I was impressed with the fact that he looked so many years younger.

One night I couldn't resist inquiring of Jack the secret of his never-changing appearance. He laughed heartily, but refused to divulge any of his "secrets."

As he ordered that evening it occurred to me that his menu selections invariably include shark's fin soup. According to Chinese belief, shark's fin soup gives a man added virility and prolonged youth.

Seaweed Soup
鉙 Gee Choy Tong 鉙

HAVE READY:
- 2 cans chicken broth
- 1 can water
- ½ cup ground pork
- 1 package seaweed (10 pieces)
- ½ cup finely chopped canned mushrooms
- ½ cup frozen peas
- ½ cup finely chopped canned water chestnuts
- 1 egg

STEP 1:

Pour the 2 cans of broth and 1 can of water into a 2-quart pot, cover and bring to a boil over high heat. When boiling, add the pork and cover, cooking over high heat for 12 minutes.

STEP 2:

While broth is boiling, tear the seaweed into small pieces, put into a bowl and cover with water to soak. When the broth has cooked for 12 minutes, drain the seaweed and add to the soup, along with the mushrooms, peas and water chestnuts. Cook uncovered for 1 minute.

STEP 3:

Slightly beat the egg in a small bowl. When the soup reaches the boiling stage, slowly pour in the egg. Stir and serve immediately.

Serves four.

Family Water Cress Soup

🔃 Sai Yueng Choy Tong 🔃

HAVE READY:
   1 bunch water cress
   2 cans chicken broth
   1 can water

METHOD:

Pick off the leaves of the water cress, discarding the stems. Bring the broth and water to a boil over high heat, and add the water cress. Keep covered, and when the broth comes to a boil again, the soup is ready. Do not remove the cover during cooking; it will turn the water cress leaves yellow.

(Note: I prefer to use the College Inn Chicken Broth, since it seems to go best with Cantonese cooking.)

54

When my son George was a little boy, he was very finicky about his food and, like many another mother, I had difficulty in trying to convince him to eat his vegetables.

One day I made some water cress soup, and it looked so attractive as I poured it into the serving bowl that George asked if he might have a taste of it.

Naturally, I was pleased when he liked his first cup so much that he asked for a second, and from that day on it was his favorite. Even when I could not find water cress at the market and made the soup with spinach, he still enjoyed it.

I mention all this because George is now 6 feet 2 inches tall, and I often wonder how much his daily portions of water cress soup had to do with it because, little by little, he began to enjoy other vegetables, too.

Bird's Nest Soup
⚛ Yin Woh Tong ⚛

HAVE READY:

4 ounces dry bird's nest	2 teaspoons cornstarch
2 quarts water	1 egg white
1 ½" slice ginger root	½ teaspoon salt
3 cans chicken broth	¾ teaspoon light
¼ cup finely chopped	Chinese soy sauce
Virginia ham	

STEP 1:

Soak the bird's nest in cold water overnight, then drain and pick out any remaining foreign matter. After cleaning, put the bird's nest with the ginger root in 1 quart boiling water, cook about ½ hour, then drain and rinse with cold water. Discard the ginger root.

STEP 2:

Put the chicken broth, bird's nest and 2 cans of water (measure with chicken broth can) and boil over a low fire for 1 hour. Then add the ham, a mixture of 2 teaspoons cornstarch with 2 teaspoons water, and beat the egg white into the soup. Just before serving, add salt and soy sauce.

Serves four.

Mae West is another famous personality who seems to have found eternal youth. Her flawless complexion is so remarkable that I could not resist asking her whether she had ever had her face lifted.

"Never," she replied, "I just follow a number of strict health rules and one of them is to have a bowl of bird's nest soup regularly."

The Chinese have long felt that Bird's Nest Soup enhances feminine charm and beauty (as shark's fin soup helps a man's virility). Mae West seems to lend credence to this ancient belief.

Champagne Coconut Soup
🔃 Heung Bun Yea Chup Tong 🔃

(Hainan Island off the southern coast of China is known for the abundance of coconuts which grow there, and quite naturally they are used in numerous ways in the local native cooking. A very popular dish is the Hainan coconut soup, to which we have added champagne.)

PREPARE COCONUTS:
4 fresh coconuts about 6 inches high

Remove the hard husk and with a saw, cut a 2-inch cap from each. Set the cap aside until ready to serve the soup. Drain and discard the coconut milk.

HAVE READY:

- 2 cans chicken broth
- 2 cans water
- 4 tablespoons diced uncooked chicken meat
- 1/4" pared slice of ginger root
- 1 teaspoon sugar
- dash pepper
- 4 ounces soaked, dried, torn Cloud Ear Fungus
- 4 tablespoons soaked, drained black mushrooms
- 4 tablespoons fresh shredded crab meat
- 2 tablespoons diced Virginia ham
- 2 tablespoons red cooking wine
- 10 drops sesame oil
- 4 ounces champagne

STEP 1:

Mix broth and water in a pot and bring to a boil. Add chicken, ginger root, sugar, pepper, Cloud Ear and mushrooms, cover and simmer for 15 minutes. Discard ginger root.

STEP 2:

Place shells on steamer tray, fill with soup mixture, crab meat and ham to about 3/4-full, then add wine and sesame oil.

STEP 3:

When water in the steamer is boiling, add the tray with shells and steam covered, over continuous boiling water, for 1 hour.

STEP 4:

Put each shell on a serving dish, add 1 ounce of champagne per shell, place on top and serve.

When my father-in-law served as Ambassador to the United States, invitations to dine at the Chinese Embassy were held in high regard in Washington, D.C. My mother-in-law was known as a very accomplished hostess who set a wonderful table.

She took a personal interest in every detail of her parties, planning and shopping for each dinner herself, and soon became a familiar figure at the market, selecting vegetables, fruits and fish.

Also, to insure their freshness, she hand-picked the chickens that went into her dinners.

On one of the first occasions when she went to the poultryman who she thought sold the best quality of fowl, she carefully chose the number of chickens she needed, then asked for a quantity of chicken wings and feet.

Up to that time, no one would buy those parts, and the poultryman had just thrown them away. So, obligingly, he filled a huge bag with wings and feet, and presented them to my mother-in-law free of charge.

Several weeks following that particular party, she went back to the poultryman to buy more fowl. Again she requested another bag of chicken feet and wings, but this time, however, he presented her with a bill for them.

He had had so many calls for them from guests at her dinner that they had now become much-desired items!

Steamed Chicken Feet & Black Mushroom Soup
卍 Dung Goo Dun Gai 卍

HAVE READY:
- ¼ pound black dried mushrooms
- 24 chicken feet (have butcher remove outer skin and nails)
- 2 cups warm water
- 2 cans chicken broth (skim off fat)
- 1 teaspoon salt
- 2 slices ginger root ¼-inch thick
- 1 tablespoon cooking wine
- ¼ cup chopped green onions and stem
- ¼ cup finely chopped ham

STEP 1:

Wash the mushrooms carefully and soak for 30 minutes in 2 cups of warm water which you will reserve for the soup. Drain by tipping the water out without disturbing the mushrooms at the bottom. Wash the mushrooms several times more under cold running water to remove any lingering sand grains. Drain and put mushrooms back into the reserved water.

STEP 2:

Put the chicken feet with the mushrooms/water, add the broth, salt and ginger root. Place in an oven-proof bowl in the steamer, and steam over boiling water for 3 hours.

STEP 3:

Remove from the steamer, sprinkle with the wine, onions and ham, and serve hot.

Serves four.

Chinese Greens Vegetable Soup
🔁 Ching Choy Tong 🔁

HAVE READY:

2 cups Chinese greens, cut diagonally
¼ cup snow peas
2 cans chicken broth
1 can water
¼ cup sliced button mushrooms
¼ cup sliced bamboo shoots
¼ cup sliced water chestnuts
½ teaspoon salt
½ teaspoon light soy sauce
½ teaspoon M.S.G. (optional)
1 drop sesame oil
1 pinch white pepper

STEP 1:

Wash greens and snow peas, and slice lengthwise, using the French diagonal cut.

STEP 2:

Combine chicken broth and water, and bring to a boil over medium heat. Now add the greens, mushrooms, bamboo shoots, snow peas and water chestnuts, and cook covered for 5 minutes. Just before serving, add the salt, light soy sauce, M.S.G., sesame oil and pepper.

Serves four in Chinese soup cups.

Seafood

'Cashew Shrimp
🔁 Yue Kwo Har Yan 🔁

HAVE READY:

1 cup uncooked shrimp (16 to a pound), cleaned, shelled, deveined and cut into thirds

1 teaspoon light soy sauce

1 teaspoon dry sherry

¼ teaspoon white pepper

1 teaspoon cornstarch

4½ tablespoons vegetable oil

½ cup diced canned bamboo shoots

½ cup toasted cashew nuts

1 slice ginger root, ¼-inch wide

2 green onions with stem, diagonally sliced into 1-inch strips

1 teaspoon salt

¼ teaspoon M.S.G. (optional)

½ teaspoon sesame oil

STEP 1:

Put the cut-up shrimp in a bowl, and sprinkle over them the soy sauce, wine, pepper, cornstarch and one tablespoon oil.

STEP 2:

In a preheated wok heat 1½ tablespoons vegetable oil. Quick-fry the bamboo shoots and cashew nuts for 1 minute. Put in a bowl and set aside.

STEP 3:

Clean and dry the wok, preheat and add 2 tablespoons oil. When hot, swirl the ginger root slice around the sides and bottom, then discard. Add the onions and shrimp, quick-fry for 2 minutes. Now add the bamboo shoots and cashew nuts and stir well. Finally add the salt, monosodium glutamate (M.S.G.) and sesame oil, stir evenly and serve.

Serves four.

Shrimp Egg Foo Yung
🜲 Har Foo Yung Dohn 🜲

HAVE READY:
- 1 cup bean sprouts, chopped
- ¼ cup chopped mushrooms
- ¼ cup cooked shrimp, chopped small
- ¼ cup white onion, chopped
- 1 teaspoon salt
- 1 teaspoon light soy sauce
- 4 eggs
- ¼ cup crisp noodles (or substitute shoestring potatoes)

METHOD:

Mix together the bean sprouts, mushrooms, shrimp, onion, salt and soy sauce, then add the eggs, mix, and finally mix in the crisp noodles.

Shape the mixture into individual patties about the size of a hamburger. Heat 1 tablespoon oil in a large frying pan or on the grill, and cook the patties for 2 minutes on each side.

Serves four.

Quick Fry Shrimp in Shell
🜲 Yau Boo Har Len Hoc 🜲

(Shrimp cooked in the shell is more tender than if it is shelled before cooking.)

HAVE READY:
- 12 fresh jumbo shrimp
- 3 tablespoons vegetable oil
- 2 cloves crushed garlic
- 2 green onions sliced diagonally
- 1 ½" ginger slice
- 2 teaspoons dark soy sauce
- 1 teaspoon light soy sauce
- 1 tablespoon cooking wine
- 1 teaspoon sugar
- ½ teaspoon salt

STEP 1:

Wash the shrimp. With a knife or a pair of scissors, open up the backs of the shrimp and pull out the black vein with a toothpick. Remove the sharp point at the tail. Dry shrimp thoroughly on paper towels.

STEP 2:

In a preheated wok or skillet, heat the oil, add the garlic, onion and ginger, stir around on bottom and sides, then discard the garlic, onion and ginger. Add shrimp one at a time, on the flat side. Quick-fry for 2 minutes, or until pink. Turn on other side, quick-fry for 2 more minutes. Add the soy sauces, wine, sugar and salt, stir evenly, remove from the fire and serve hot.

Serves four.

Crabmeat & Brussel Sprouts
🔁 Hai Yoke Chow Yea Choy Tsai 🔁

HAVE READY:

12 brussel sprouts or ½-head of cabbage cut into the size of brussel sprouts	crabmeat, drained and dried on paper toweling
4 tablespoons vegetable oil	1 teaspoon cooking wine
1 teaspoon salt	1 teaspoon cornstarch blended with 1 tablespoon water
½ can chicken broth	
1 1-inch slice ginger root, crushed	
1 clove garlic, crushed	1 egg white, unbeaten
1 cup fresh or canned	1 green onion and stem, chopped

STEP 1:

Using sufficient water to cover the brussel sprouts, bring to a boil and add sprouts. Boil for 3 minutes. Drain and dry on paper towels. Set aside.

STEP 2:
    In a preheated wok, heat 2 tablespoons oil.
Add ¼-can broth, sprouts, salt, and stir-fry for
2 minutes. Using a slotted spoon to drain off
liquid, put the sprouts on a platter.

STEP 3:
    Wash, dry and preheat wok. Heat 2 tablespoons
of oil, swirl in ginger and garlic around bottom
and sides, then discard the ginger and garlic. Add
the crabmeat and sprinkle the wine over it. Stir
for one minute, then pour in the remaining
¼-cup broth and bring to a boil. Blend in the
cornstarch mixture, stirring to a smooth texture.
Stir in the egg white. Pour this mixture over the
brussel sprouts and garnish with the green onion.
Serve immediately.

    Serves four.

Lemon Fish
🔁 Ning Mon Yue 🔁

HAVE READY:

½ cup cornstarch	4½ teaspoons sugar
½ cup all-purpose flour	(or 2 tablespoons
1 teaspoon baking	honey)
powder	2 teaspoons
1 cup water	cornstarch
2 quarts vegetable oil	blended with 2
2 pieces filet of sole	tablespoons
(about 1 pound)	water
3 tablespoons fresh	1 sprig parsley
lemon juice	4 maraschino cherries

STEP 1:
    Make a batter of ½-cup cornstarch, the all-
purpose flour, baking powder, 1 cup water and
1 teaspoon vegetable oil. Blend well.

STEP 2:

Heat 2 quarts vegetable oil in the wok (about 350° F.). Drop the filet of sole into the batter and cover completely. Slip into the oil for 2 minutes, until light golden brown, then remove and drain on paper toweling.

STEP 3:

Mix together the lemon juice, 4½ teaspoons of sugar and a blend of 2 teaspoons cornstarch with 2 tablespoons water, bring to a boil and pour over the fish. Garnish with parsley and cherry, and serve immediately.

Serves four.

When I entertained the former Chinese Consul General in Los Angeles, I served this dish. He was a gourmet cook himself, and told me later that he had prepared the fish at home and it came out so well that he featured it at a dinner party he gave for the entire Los Angeles Consular Corps.

Swimming Sea Bass
🔁 Sang Mun Hai Lei 🔁

HAVE READY:

1 2½–3 pound sea bass (Leave head and tail intact. Remove points from fins. Clean inside and out with a little salt. Rinse well and put on a platter.)	cut into 1½-inch diagonal slices
	4 tablespoons vegetable oil
	2 teaspoons light soy sauce
	1 tablespoon dark soy sauce
3 quarts water	½ teaspoon salt
¼ cup thin-sliced ginger	1 teaspoon cooking sherry
¼ cup green onion,	

STEP 1:

Place a perforated rack in a turkey roaster long enough for the fish. Bring 3 quarts of water to a rolling boil. Slide the fish into the water in the roaster, and cover with the lid. Return to a boil, and boil for one minute. Turn off the heat and let sit for 15 minutes, covered. Then carefully remove the fish rack from the roaster and slide the fish onto a serving platter. Arrange the ginger and onion slices over the fish, covering it completely.

STEP 2:
Preheat the wok until very hot, then heat the vegetable oil. When very hot, pour it slowly over the fish, so that the ginger and onion flavor will permeate the fish. Finally pour over it a mixture of the soy sauces, salt and sherry, and serve immediately.

Serves four.

Jade Fish
🔁 Bak Lok Yue 🔁

HAVE READY:

1 whole sea bass, about 1½–2 pounds water	4 green onions with 6-inches of stem
½ head iceberg or romaine lettuce, shredded	2 teaspoons soy sauce
	1 tablespoon oyster sauce
4 tablespoons vegetable oil	1 teaspoon vinegar
1 cup Chinese pea pods	½ teaspoon salt
1 cup mushrooms, thin-sliced	½ teaspoon sugar
12 pieces ginger root, cut into matchstick strips	2 teaspoons cornstarch blended with 4 tablespoons water

STEP 1:
Clean and scale the fish, leaving the head and tail on. Dry and salt lightly inside and out. Place

the fish in a wok with boiling water up to one-half the thickness of the fish. Cover and simmer for 10 to 15 minutes, until the flesh flakes easily with a fork.

STEP 2:

Line a platter with the shredded lettuce and lift out fish carefully with a slotted spatula. Place on lettuce and set aside. Save the fish broth.

STEP 3:

Heat the 4 tablespoons of oil in the wok, add pea pods and quick-fry for a few seconds until they turn bright green, remove and set aside. Now add the mushrooms to the oil and fry until tender. Add the fish broth, ginger, green onions, soy sauce, oyster sauce, vinegar, salt and sugar, and bring to a boil. Pour in the cornstarch blend and stir until the mixture is thick and smooth. Now put in the pea pods, reheat and arrange the pods around the fish. Just before serving, pour over the remaining sauce.

Serves four.

Sweet & Sour Whole Fish
🔁 Teem Suen Yue 🔁

HAVE READY:

1 sea bass or red snapper, 1½–2 pounds	3 tablespoons sugar
salt	red food coloring
1 beaten egg	1 cup green pepper, cut in chunks
1 cup flour	½ cup white onion, cut in chunks
vegetable oil	½ cup canned diced pineapple
1 cup water	
½ cup catsup	1 teaspoon cornstarch blended with
2 tablespoons white vinegar	1 tablespoon water

PREPARE FISH:

Clean and scale the fish, leaving the head and tail on. Dry and salt inside and out, and make 3 slashes ¼" deep on each side for better cooking. Brush the fish with the beaten egg, then roll in the flour which has been spread on a platter.

STEP 1:

Pour enough vegetable oil to a depth of 3 inches in a roasting pan and heat to 375° F., testing by dropping in a cube of bread. If it comes to the surface immediately and browns, the oil is ready.

STEP 2:

First immerse the head in the oil very gently so that there is no splatter, then slide in the rest of the fish. Deep-fry from 3 to 5 minutes on each side, remove and drain on a paper towel, then place on a platter.

PREPARE SAUCE:

Prepare the sweet and sour sauce by bringing 1 cup water, the catsup, 1 tablespoon oil, vinegar, sugar and a few drops of the food coloring to a boil in a wok or skillet. Then add the green pepper and onion; bring to a boil. Boil for 1 minute, then add the pineapple and again bring to a boil and stir in the cornstarch blend to thicken the sauce.

STEP 3:

Pour the sauce over the fish and serve immediately so that the fish does not become soggy.

Serves four.

Glass Shrimp With Peas
🔁 Ching Tau Bo Lei Har Kow 🔁

HAVE READY:

- 2 quarts water
- 2 cups frozen peas
- 1 tablespoon vegetable oil
- 1 ¼" slice of ginger root
- ¼ cup green onion, sliced diagonally
- 1 cup uncooked shrimp, deveined and cut in half
- 1 teaspoon salt
- ¼ teaspoon pepper
- 1 teaspoon cornstarch blended with 1 tablespoon water
- ½ teaspoon sesame oil

METHOD:

Bring 2 quarts of water to a boil, add the peas, bring to a boil again, then drain peas and set aside. Preheat the wok or skillet, and coat bottom and sides with 1 tablespoon oil. Add the piece of ginger, rubbing it on the sides and bottom, then discard the ginger. Quick-fry the onions briefly, then the shrimp. When the shrimp turn pink, they are cooked, so be careful not to overcook. Season with salt and pepper. Stir in the cornstarch blend and the peas, and just before serving add the sesame oil, stir and serve.

Serves four.

Lobster Cantonese
🔁 Kwong Chaw Lung Har 🔁

HAVE READY:

2 tablespoons vegetable oil
1 clove garlic
2 tablespoons pre-served black soy-beans mashed together with 2 cloves garlic
¼ pound ground lean pork
2 cups uncooked lobster tails, cut in small chunks
¼ teaspoon salt
dash pepper
1 tablespoon dark Chinese soy sauce
1 teaspoon light Chinese soy sauce
½ cup water
1 teaspoon red cooking wine
1 teaspoon cornstarch blended with 2 tablespoons water
1 egg

STEP 1:

Swirl oil around bottom and sides of a preheated wok or skillet. When hot, add the clove of garlic, rub around bottom and sides, and discard garlic. Add the black bean and garlic mash, the pork, and stir for 3 or 4 minutes over high heat. Then add the lobster and stir-fry 1 or 2 minutes until the lobster turns pink.

STEP 2:

Add salt, pepper, soy sauces and wine. Stir 1 minute, then add water, stir and bring to a boil. When boiling, add the cornstarch blend and stir well. Just before removing from the fire, add the unbeaten egg, stir and serve.

Serves four.

Abalone with Oyster Sauce

🔁 Hao Yau Bao Yue 🔁

HAVE READY:

3 tablespoons vegetable oil
½ head lettuce
1 teaspoon salt
½ cup chicken broth
1 teaspoon cornstarch blended with
  2 tablespoons water
3 teaspoons oyster sauce
½ teaspoon dark soy sauce
¼ teaspoon sugar
1 can abalone, thin-sliced
½ cup pea pods
1 drop sesame oil

STEP 1:

Preheat the wok and swirl 2 tablespoons vegetable oil around bottom and sides. Cut the lettuce into 4 pieces and quick-fry with 1 teaspoon salt and ½ cup of chicken broth for 2 or 3 minutes, until soft. Drain and set aside on a plate.

STEP 2:

Using the same wok, add 1 tablespoon vegetable oil, the cornstarch blend, oyster sauce, soy sauce and sugar. Stir until boiling, then add abalone slices, pea pods and sesame oil, and cook for 1 minute.

To serve, spoon over prepared lettuce.

Serves four.

Cantonese Shrimp with Black Bean Sauce
🔁 Kwong Chaw Dow See Har Kow 🔁

HAVE READY:

2 tablespoons vegetable oil

2 tablespoons preserved black soybeans put through a garlic press with 2 peeled cloves of garlic

¼ pound ground lean pork (optional)

2 cups uncooked shrimp, cleaned, peeled, deveined

and butterfly-cut in half

1 teaspoon red cooking wine

½ teaspoon salt

¼ cup water

1 tablespoon dark Chinese soy sauce

1 unbeaten egg

1 teaspoon cornstarch blended with 2 tablespoons water

STEP 1:

Swirl oil around bottom and sides of wok or skillet. Quick-fry over high heat the black bean and garlic mash, and the pork; cook for 5 minutes. Now add the shrimp and quick-fry 2 minutes more, then add the wine, salt, water, soy sauce and unbeaten egg, stirring thoroughly.

STEP 2:

Make a nest in the center of the wok, pour in the cornstarch blend and stir.

Serve hot immediately.

Serves four.

Sweet & Sour Fried Shrimp
🔁 Jar Teem Suen Har 🔁

HAVE READY:

1 cup all-purpose flour
½ cup cornstarch
1 teaspoon baking powder
1 teaspoon salt
1 egg
2 cups water
1 quart vegetable oil
16 shrimp, size 16/20, washed, shelled, deveined and butterfly-cut
½ cup catsup
2 tablespoons white vinegar
3 tablespoons sugar
1 dash red food coloring
1 cup green pepper, cut into chunks
½ cup white onion, cut into chunks
½ cup canned pineapple slices, cut in chunks

STEP 1:

In a bowl, mix a batter of the flour, ¼-cup cornstarch, baking powder, salt, 1 teaspoon vegetable oil, the egg, and 1 cup of water. Blend to the consistency of a thin ribbon of liquid.

STEP 2:

Heat 1 quart of vegetable oil in a deep-fryer to 375° F. Dip the shrimp into the batter, letting the excess drip back into the bowl. Slip the shrimp into the hot oil, let it fry until golden brown (1 or 2 minutes). Drain on a paper towel. Fry only 2 or 3 shrimp at a time.

STEP 3:

Into a wok or skillet, mix 1 cup of water, the catsup, 1 teaspoon vegetable oil, vinegar, sugar and food coloring. Bring it to a boil over medium heat. Then add the green pepper chunks and the white onion, and bring to a boil. Stir-boil 1 minute. Add the pineapple and return to a boil. In a separate bowl blend 1 teaspoon cornstarch with 1 tablespoon water and add it to the mixture in order to thicken the sauce.

Add the deep-fried shrimp, stir and remove immediately from the heat to a platter and serve.

Serves four generously.

Steamed Whole Fish
🔃 Jing Yue 🔃

HAVE READY:
- 1 whole sea bass, 1½–2 pounds, cleaned, scaled with head intact
- 1 green onion with 6 inches of stem, divided into 3-inch long pieces, then diagonally thin-sliced
- 1 ¼" piece of ginger root, pared and cut into thin strips
- salt
- 3 tablespoons vegetable oil
- 1 teaspoon light Chinese soy sauce
- 1 tablespoon dark Chinese soy sauce

STEP 1:
Wash and dry the fish, and butterfly cut along the underside. Slash about 3 times on each side, about ¼-inch deep, to help cook evenly. Lightly salt inside and out, and put on a platter which can be placed in a steamer. Arrange the onion and ginger slices diagonally across the slashes on the fish, creating a pattern for aesthetic appearance.

STEP 2:
When the bottom section of the steamer is boiling, place the platter in the section above the water, cover and steam for 10 minutes. You can use a roasting pan, placing the platter on a rack, but be sure that the water does not come up to the platter. Cover and steam for 10 minutes.

STEP 3:
Just before serving, heat 3 tablespoons of vegetable oil and pour over the fish, then sprinkle on the soy sauces.

Serves four.

Chicken Dishes

Ants Climb the Tree

Ma Ngi Sheun Shee

HAVE READY:

- **½ package bean threads (about ½ pound)**
- **½ pound ground uncooked chicken**
- **3 tablespoons vegetable oil**
- **1 teaspoon light soy sauce**
- **1 tablespoon dark soy sauce**
- **1 teaspoon cooking wine**
- **½ teaspoon sugar**
- **1 tablespoon cornstarch**
- **¼ teaspoon sesame oil**
- **1 tablespoon thin-sliced green onion**
- **1 cup chicken broth**

PREPARE THE DAY BEFORE:

Soak the bean threads in cold water overnight. Marinate the chicken in a blend of 1 tablespoon oil, the soy sauces, wine, sugar, cornstarch and sesame oil. Refrigerate overnight.

METHOD:

In the wok, heat 2 tablespoons oil, quick-fry the green onions for a few seconds, then put in the chicken marinade, stirring for 5 minutes. Now add the drained bean threads and 1 cup chicken broth, stir for 1 more minute, then serve.

Serves four.

Sweet & Sour Chicken

Teem Suen Gai

HAVE READY:

- **2 quarts vegetable oil**
- **1 cup boned, uncooked chicken breast, cut into 1″ pieces**

HAVE READY FOR BATTER:
- ½ cup all-purpose flour
- ¼ cup cornstarch
- ½ teaspoon baking powder
- ¼ teaspoon salt
- ¾ cup water

STEP 1:

In a bowl, mix dry ingredients with water and stir until the batter is the consistency of a smooth, thin stream.

STEP 2:

Heat the vegetable oil in a large kettle until it is very hot (375° F.). Then dip the chicken pieces into the batter, one at a time, letting the excess batter drip back into the bowl. Put them in a few at a time in the hot oil and deep-fry for 5 minutes. Drain on paper toweling and set aside.

HAVE READY FOR SAUCE:
- ¾ cup catsup
- ¼ cup white vinegar
- 3 tablespoons sugar
- 1 can pineapple chunks with juice
- ½ cup chopped white onion
- ½ cup chopped green pepper
- 1 tablespoon cornstarch blended with 2 tablespoons water

STEP 3:

In a bowl, blend the catsup, vinegar, sugar and pineapple juice. Pour this mix into a pre-heated wok or skillet, and bring to a boil over high heat. When it begins boiling, add the onion and peppers, and again return to a boil. Now add the cornstarch blend, stir and add the pineapple chunks. When this mixture again reaches the boiling stage, add the deep-fried chicken, stir in well and serve immediately.

Serves four.

Chicken Asparagus
↺ Lo Suhn Chow Gai ↺

HAVE READY:

2 cups uncooked white chicken meat, thin-sliced

5½ tablespoons vegetable oil

2 teaspoons salt

1 teaspoon light soy sauce

1½ tablespoons cornstarch

2 tablespoons salted black beans, washed in cold water

3 cloves garlic, peeled and crushed

4 cups fresh asparagus, diagonally sliced

¼ cup chicken broth

½ teaspoon sugar

1 tablespoon dark soy sauce

MARINATE OVERNIGHT:

Marinate the chicken overnight with 1 tablespoon vegetable oil, 1 teaspoon of salt, 1 teaspoon of light soy sauce, and 1 tablespoon cornstarch. Mix well.

STEP 1:

Mix together the black beans, garlic and ½ teaspoon oil. Heat 2 tablespoons oil in the wok and put in the black bean mixture and the asparagus. Stir well, then add 1 teaspoon chicken broth, 1 teaspoon salt and ½ teaspoon sugar. Stir-fry for about 5 minutes, until crisp but not overdone. Set aside on a platter.

STEP 2:

Heat the wok again with 2 tablespoons oil and quick-fry the chicken about 3 minutes. Then add the dark soy sauce, a blend of ¼ cup chicken broth with 1 teaspoon cornstarch. Stir thoroughly, then mix in the asparagus mixture and remove from fire.

Serves four.

Kung Bow Chicken
🀁 Kung Bow Gai Ding 🀁

HAVE READY:

- 1 cup uncooked chicken, diced
- 3 tablespoons vegetable oil
- 1 teaspoon light soy sauce
- 1½ tablespoons dark soy sauce
- 1 teaspoon cornstarch
- 1 clove crushed garlic
- 1 cup green pepper cut into ½-inch pieces
- 1 cup diced canned bamboo shoots
- 1 tablespoon chopped peanuts
- ½ cup black mushrooms, diced (soak for 15 minutes in hot water, rinse and drain)
- 1 piece (1 inch long) dry red hot pepper, or 1 or 2 teaspoons Chinese chili paste with garlic—depending on how hot you prefer your dish
- ¼ teaspoon monosodium glutamate (M.S.G., optional)

STEP 1:

Marinate the diced chicken with 1 tablespoon oil, 1 teaspoon light soy sauce, 1 teaspoon dark soy sauce and 1 teaspoon cornstarch.

STEP 2:

In a preheated wok, heat 2 tablespoons oil. Swirl garlic clove over the bottom and sides, then discard. Add the marinated chicken, stir and cook for 1 minute. Now add the green pepper, bamboo shoots, peanuts and mushrooms with 1 tablespoon dark soy sauce and the hot pepper. Stir and cook 2 minutes. Add the monosodium glutamate and stir for 1 minute. Turn off the flame and serve immediately.

Serves four.

Chicken Wings with Oyster Sauce
卍 Hao Yao Gai Yik 卍

HAVE READY:

3 tablespoons vegetable
  oil
2 cloves crushed garlic
8 chicken wings
2 tablespoons dark
  soy sauce

1 teaspoon light
  Chinese soy sauce
3 tablespoons oyster
  sauce
½ cup water
1 tablespoon sugar

STEP 1:

First divide each chicken wing into 3 parts, wash
and dry off. Then preheat the wok and coat
bottom and sides with 3 tablespoons oil. Coat
the bottom and sides with garlic, discarding the
cloves when they turn black. Add the middle and
tip parts of the wings, brown on both sides, then
add the bottom third and brown.

STEP 2:

Mix the soy sauces and oyster sauce into the
chicken, then stir in the water and sugar. Cover
and cook over medium heat for 15 minutes.
Serve hot.

Serves four.

Chicken with Plum Sauce
🔁 Suen Mui Chien Gai 🔁

MARINATE:

2 cups uncooked, boned breast of chicken, cut into ½-inch by 1-inch pieces
1 teaspoon vegetable oil
½ teaspoon salt
1 tablespoon dark soy sauce
½ teaspoon sugar
1 teaspoon red cooking wine
1 teaspoon cornstarch

HAVE READY:

3 tablespoons vegetable oil
2 cloves garlic, crushed but whole
½ cup canned whole button mushrooms
½ cup thin-sliced canned bamboo shoots
½ cup thin-sliced canned water chestnuts
1 scant teaspoon cornstarch, blended with 1 tablespoon water
1 tablespoon plum sauce
1 tablespoon Hoisin sauce
½ teaspoon sesame oil

STEP 1:

In a preheated wok, coat bottom and sides with 3 tablespoons vegetable oil. Then rub the bottom and sides with garlic cloves, remove and discard the garlic. Add the marinated chicken, quick-fry for about 5 minutes, not stirring too much or it will get watery. Add mushrooms, bamboo shoots and chestnuts, and saute for about 2 or 3 minutes.

STEP 2:

Mix the cornstarch and water in a bowl, then add the plum sauce and Hoisin sauce. Make a nest in the chicken mixture, add the cornstarch and sauces and stir through the chicken/vegetable mixture. Just before serving, add the sesame oil and remove from the fire into a platter. Serve hot immediately.

Serves four.

Cantonese Chicken Chow Mein

⚵ Kwang Chaw Gai Chow Mein ⚵

HAVE READY:

8 ounces Chinese noodles (or thin spaghetti)
water
5 tablespoons vegetable oil
1/4" slice ginger root, pared
1 cup boned, uncooked chicken, cut into strips
1/4 teaspoon salt
2 teaspoons light soy sauce
1 teaspoon dark soy sauce

1 cup Chinese black mushrooms, cut into strips, but first washed and soaked for 15 minutes (substitute canned mushrooms)
4 heaping cups Chinese cabbage, sliced into 2-inch strips
1 cup cooked ham, cut into strips

STEP 1:

Immerse the noodles or spaghetti in boiling water, cover and cook over high heat for 15 minutes. Drain under cold water. Add 1 tablespoon vegetable oil to keep the noodles separated. Set aside. Should make 3 heaping cupsful.

STEP 2:

Coat the bottom and sides of a preheated wok or skillet with 2 tablespoons vegetable oil. Add the ginger root, coat bottom and sides, then discard the root. Now quick-fry the chicken, uncovered, for 3 minutes. Add the salt, 1 teaspoon light soy sauce and the mushrooms. Next stir in the Chinese cabbage and 1/4 cup water; cover and quick-fry for 5 minutes. Add the ham, stirring it in thoroughly. Remove the chicken/ham mixture to a bowl and set aside.

STEP 3:

Preheat the wok or skillet and coat with 2 tablespoons oil. Quick-fry the noodles or spaghetti for 3 minutes, then add 1 tablespoon dark soy sauce and 1 teaspoon light soy sauce, stir and mix in thoroughly. Add the chicken/ham mixture, stir well and serve hot.

Serves four generously.

Yangchow Chicken Chow Mein
🔃 Yueng Chaw Gai Chow Mein 🔃

HAVE READY:

water

8 ounces Chinese noodles

6½ tablespoons vegetable oil

1 cup uncooked chicken, skinned, boned and thin-sliced

2 tablespoons dark soy sauce

1 teaspoon light soy sauce

2 teaspoons cornstarch

1 crushed garlic clove

1 cup black mushrooms, soaked for 15 minutes, drained and thin-sliced

4½ cups celery cabbage, shredded

4 tablespoons chicken broth

1 cup shredded canned bamboo shoots

¼ cup canned preserved turnips, soaked 30 minutes in cold water, rinsed well to remove excess salt, thin-sliced

¼ teaspoon monosodium glutamate (optional)

½ cup thin-sliced canned abalone

STEP 1:

Bring the water to boil in a 2-quart kettle. When boiling, drop in the noodles, cover and cook over a high heat for 15 minutes. Drain in a colander and rinse in cold water. Return to the kettle, pour in 1 tablespoon vegetable oil to keep the noodles separated. Set aside.

STEP 2:

To the chicken pieces, add 1 teaspoon oil, 1 tablespoon dark soy sauce, 1 teaspoon light soy sauce and 2 teaspoons cornstarch.

STEP 3:

Preheat the wok. Heat 3 tablespoons oil and when hot, swirl the garlic clove around sides and bottom, then discard. Add the chicken mixture and quick-fry for 2 minutes. Add the mushrooms and mix for 1 minute. Add the celery cabbage, stirring for 2 minutes. Stir in the broth and cook for 2 minutes, then add the bamboo shoots, turnips and monosodium glutamate, and stir. Turn off the fire and add the abalone. Set aside in the wok.

STEP 4:

Heat skillet and add 2 tablespoons oil. When hot, stir in the cooked noodles with 1 tablespoon dark soy sauce. Mix well and pour into a platter. Over the noodles, spoon the chicken mixture and serve immediately.

Serves four, generously.

Fun See Chicken
🔃 Fun See Gai 🔃

PREPARE AHEAD:
   ¼ **package Fun See (vermicelli)** soaked in cold water for 20 minutes. Drain off the water. You may store this in the refrigerator ahead of time.

MARINATE CHICKEN:
   1 **cup thin-sliced boned, uncooked dark chicken meat**
   ½ **teaspoon vegetable oil**
   ½ **teaspoon cornstarch**
   1 **tablespoon dark Chinese soy sauce**
   1 **teaspoon light Chinese soy sauce**

THIN-SLICE:
  ½ cup canned bamboo shoots
  ½ cup Chinese black mushrooms, soaked for
      15 minutes
  1 cup white Chinese cabbage (or American cabbage)
  ½ cup fresh pea pods

HAVE READY:
  1 clove crushed garlic
  2 cups water
  ¼ teaspoon M.S.G. (optional)
  ¼ teaspoon sugar (optional)
  3 tablespoons vegetable oil

STEP 1:
  Preheat wok or skillet. Add 3 tablespoons oil,
  coating sides and bottom. Add garlic clove,
  coating bottom and sides, remove and discard the
  garlic. Add the marinated chicken and quick-fry
  over high heat for 3 minutes. Then add the black
  mushrooms and saute for 1 minute. Now add
  the cabbage, stir-fry for 2 minutes, then the
  bamboo shoots, stir for 1 minute. Add the water,
  cover and bring to a boil, and add the 2 cups
  dried Fun See, stir well. Cover for 1 minute.

STEP 2:
  Remove the cover, add the pea pods and stir-fry
  for 1 minute. Finally add the M.S.G. and sugar,
  stir in, and immediately take off the fire. Put
  into a serving dish and serve without delay.

  Makes four generous portions.

Sizzling Go Ba
🔁 Go Ba 🔁

STEP 1:
  Go Ba is the layer of rice about ¼-inch thick
  which is formed by cooking rice 10 minutes
  longer than usual (about 20-25 minutes). For four
  people, use a wide-bottom kettle or a wok. First

spoon out the uncongealed rice, then carefully
lift out the Go Ba and set aside. It does not
matter if it breaks into pieces.

HAVE READY:
  1 cup uncooked white chicken meat chunks
  1 teaspoon vegetable oil
  1 teaspoon light soy sauce
  1 teaspoon cornstarch

STEP 2:
Marinate the chicken meat chunks with 1 teaspoon vegetable oil, 1 teaspoon light soy sauce,
and 1 teaspoon cornstarch for 10 minutes.

HAVE READY:

3 tablespoons vegetable oil	½ cup pea pods
1 cup bak choi or cabbage (Chinese or American)	½ cup sliced water chestnuts
1 teaspoon light Chinese soy sauce	½ cup canned button mushrooms
½ cup water	¼ cup cooked ham
½ cup fresh shrimp, cleaned, deveined and sliced in halves	1 teaspoon salt
	¼ teaspoon M.S.G. (optional)

STEP 3:
Swirl the vegetable oil over the bottom and sides
of the wok. When oil is hot, quick-fry the
marinated chicken over high heat for 2 or 3
minutes. Then stir in the bak choi, soy sauce and
water, cover and cook 1 or 2 minutes. Now stir
in the shrimp, then the pea pods, water chestnuts, mushrooms, ham and salt. Add the M.S.G.
last, remove from fire and set aside.

HAVE READY:
  1 quart vegetable oil

STEP 4:
Heat 1 quart vegetable oil in a deep fryer until it
is very hot (375° F.). While the oil is heating, put
a sizzling steak platter in the oven and heat it

until it sizzles when a few drops of water are
splattered on it. When oil is ready, deep-fry the
Go Ba for a few seconds on each side.

STEP 5:
Now set the platter on a wooden tray and bring
it to the serving area along with the quick-fried
meat and vegetables. Quickly place the Go Ba
on the platter, then add the vegetables and
enjoy the sizzling performance.

Serves four generously.

Lychee Chicken
🔁 Ly Gee Gai 🔁

HAVE READY:
    2 quarts vegetable oil
    1 cup boned, uncooked chicken breast, cut into
        1-inch chunks

HAVE READY FOR BATTER:
    ½ cup all-purpose flour
    ¼ cup cornstarch
    ½ teaspoon baking powder
    ¼ teaspoon salt
    ¾ cup water

STEP 1:
In a bowl, mix dry ingredients with water and stir
until the batter is the consistency of a smooth,
thin stream.

STEP 2:
Heat the vegetable oil in a large kettle until it is
very hot (375° F.). Then dip the chicken chunks
into the batter, one at a time, letting the excess
batter drip back into the bowl. Put them a
few at a time in the hot oil and deep-fry for
5 minutes. Drain on paper toweling and set aside.

HAVE READY FOR SAUCE:
- ¾ cup catsup
- ¼ cup white vinegar
- 1 cup juice from can of lychee
- 3 tablespoons sugar
- 1 can lychees with juice
- 1 cup pineapple chunks
- ½ cup chopped white onion
- ½ cup chopped green pepper
- 1 tablespoon cornstarch blended with 3 tablespoons water

STEP 3:

In a bowl, blend the catsup, vinegar, lychee juice and sugar. Pour the mixture in a pre-heated wok or large skillet and bring to a boil over high heat. When it begins boiling, add the onion and pepper, and again return to a boil. Now add the cornstarch mixture, return to a boil, then add the lychee and pineapple. When this mixture again reaches the boiling stage, add the deep-fried chicken chunks, stir in well and serve immediately.

Serves four.

Tossed Shredded Chicken Salad
🀄 Sao See Gai 🀄

PREPARE:
- **2 chicken breasts or 2 drumstick-thighs** (put in a pot, cover with water, bring to a boil and simmer for 20 minutes; remove and drain on paper toweling)

HAVE READY FOR DEEP-FRY:
- 2 quarts vegetable oil
- 8 squares wonton dough cut into ⅛" strips
- ⅓ package rice noodles
  chicken (prepared as above)

STEP 1:

Pour the 2 quarts of oil into a deep fryer and heat to 350° F. Test for readiness by dropping one of the rice noodles into the oil. If it sinks to the bottom, the oil is not hot enough. When it pops up immediately, put in the dough strips and fry to a light tan color. Remove and drain on a paper towel.

STEP 2:
Divide the noodles into three parts and deep-fry separately. The noodles should "explode" on contact with the hot oil, and should be instantly removed before the oil is absorbed. Drain on paper toweling.

STEP 3:
Now deep-fry the chicken meat for 5 minutes. Remove, drain on toweling, bone and cut into strips, including the skin. Makes 2 cups.

HAVE READY:
½ head lettuce (shred and then bed on a platter)

HAVE READY FOR CHICKEN SALAD:

2 cups cooked chicken meat	3 tablespoons toasted almonds, chopped fine
1 teaspoon liquid mustard	½ cup thinly sliced green onions, using only bulb and white stem
¼ teaspoon Five-Spice powder (optional)	
1 teaspoon sesame oil	½ teaspoon salt
2 tablespoons light soy sauce	

STEP 4:
Put the chicken meat in a large bowl. Add the mustard, Five-Spice powder, sesame oil, soy sauce, almonds, green onions, salt and mix well.

STEP 5:
Add the crisp-fried wonton strips and noodles, and mix thoroughly. They will break into small bits by the mixing. Pile the salad over the lettuce bed but do not toss; it will become soggy.

Serves four.

Deep Fried Chicken with Black Mushrooms & Pea Pods

ꖉ Hung Siu Gai Kow *ꖉ*

PREPARE:
  1 cup uncooked boned chicken breast cut into
     1-inch squares

HAVE READY FOR BATTER:
  2 quarts vegetable oil
  ½ cup all-purpose flour
  ¼ cup cornstarch
  ½ teaspoon baking powder
  ¼ teaspoon salt
  ¾ cup water

STEP 1:
  Mix flour, cornstarch, baking powder, salt and
  water, and stir until the batter is the consistency
  of a smooth, thin stream. Dip the chicken
  squares one at a time into the batter, letting the
  excess drip back into the batter bowl. Heat the
  vegetable oil in a large kettle until it is very hot
  (375° F.). Drop each square of chicken batter into
  the hot oil and deep-fry until it turns a golden
  brown and floats to the top of the oil. Take out,
  drain on a paper towel and set aside.

HAVE READY:

½ cup black Chinese mushrooms, measured after being washed and soaked for 20 minutes in hot water, OR	½ cup fresh pea pods
	½ cup canned bamboo shoots
	½ cup chopped celery
	1 ¼" slice fresh ginger root
½ cup canned button mushrooms (substitute for black mushrooms)	¼ teaspoon M.S.G. (optional)
	½ teaspoon salt
	1 teaspoon sugar
½ cup sliced canned water chestnuts	1 tablespoon oyster sauce
	3 tablespoons water
1 teaspoon cornstarch	

STEP 2:
Swirl 1 tablespoon vegetable oil around the bottom and sides of a preheated wok or skillet. Stir-fry the ginger slice to flavor the oil, then discard the ginger. Stir in the mushrooms, water chestnuts, bamboo shoots and celery, and quick-fry 2 minutes more. Stir in the salt, ½ teaspoon sugar and the M.S.G. Now add the pea pods and mix for 1 minute, then add the deep-fried chicken chunks.

STEP 3:
Blend into a smooth paste the oyster sauce, ½ teaspoon sugar, 1 teaspoon cornstarch and 3 tablespoons water. Make a well in the center of the chicken/vegetable mixture where the wok is the hottest and pour in the cornstarch paste, stir well to mix thoroughly, then serve.

Serves four generously.

Steamed Chicken with Chinese Sausages
🔁 Lap Cheon Jing Gai 🔁

HAVE READY:

2 cups uncooked boneless chicken, cut into ½-inch by 2-inch pieces	1 teaspoon cornstarch
	2½ teaspoons water
	¼ teaspoon sugar
1 tablespoon vegetable oil	2 Chinese sausages, thin-sliced diagonally
1 teaspoon thin Chinese soy sauce	

STEP 1:
In a coolie bowl or a Pyrex bowl which can be put into a steamer, mix the chicken with the oil, soy sauce, cornstarch, water and sugar. Either mix in the sausages or place on top.

Place the bowl in a steamer containing 2 inches of boiling water, cover, cook at high heat for 15 minutes, then reduce heat and cook for another 15 minutes.

Serves four.

Almond Chicken
🜲 Hung Yan Gai Ding 🜲

PREPARE:
   1 cup uncooked chicken, boned and cubed

MARINATE WITH:
   1 tablespoon vegetable oil
   ¼ teaspoon salt
   ½ teaspoon light soy sauce
       pinch of sugar (optional)

HAVE READY:

   3 tablespoons vegetable oil
   ½ cup canned or frozen peas
   ½ cup diced celery
   ½ cup sliced canned mushroom pieces
   ½ cup canned diced bamboo shoots
   ½ teaspoon salt

   1 clove garlic or ½" piece fresh ginger root
   2 tablespoons water
   2 teaspoons cornstarch blended with 3 teaspoons water
   ½ cup toasted almond halves

STEP 1:
Preheat wok or large skillet. Coat sides and bottom with 2 tablespoons vegetable oil. Quick-fry celery for 2 minutes over high heat. Add peas, mushrooms, bamboo shoots and salt. Stir for 2 minutes, then turn off heat.

STEP 2:
Preheat another skillet. Coat sides and bottom with 1 tablespoon vegetable oil, always cooking over high heat. Rub the garlic clove or ginger

root over the surfaces, then discard the garlic or ginger. Add the marinated chicken; stir for 5 minutes. Then add the cooked vegetables and 2 tablespoons water, mixing well. Pour the corn-starch blend into the mixture, stir and cook for 4 minutes. Just before serving, mix in the almond halves.

Serves four, generously.

Jade Chicken
🔃 Yuk Lan Gai 🔃

HAVE READY:

- 1 3-pound whole chicken (fresh, not frozen)
- 1 teaspoon salt
- 2 green onions with stems
- 2 quarts water
- 2 ¼" slices pared ginger root
- 1 ½-pound cooked Virginia ham (available in Chinese markets or substitute cooked canned ham)
- 2 pounds Chinese broccoli (can sub-stitute American type)
- ½ teaspoon baking soda
- 3 tablespoons vege-table oil
- 1 teaspoon sugar
- 1 teaspoon thin Chinese soy sauce
- 1 teaspoon white cooking wine
- 1 tablespoon corn-starch
- 1½ cups reserved chicken stock

STEP 1:
Wash the chicken inside and out, dry. Salt the inside cavity evenly. Tie a knot in each onion with its own stem and place the onions inside the cavity.

STEP 2:
Bring 2 quarts of water to boil in a large kettle, and when boiling, put in the chicken, breast-side

down, with the ginger root. When the water again reaches the boiling stage, reduce to low heat, cover the pot and simmer for 30 minutes. Then turn breast-up, cover and simmer for 10 minutes. Test by poking a fork into the drumstick: if it comes out dry, the chicken is done.

STEP 3:

Take the chicken out of the water and set aside to cool. Reserve the stock for later use. The boiled chicken must be very cold so that it can be boned. After boning, leaving the skin intact, cut into thin slices about 2 inches by 1 inch.

STEP 4:

On a heated oval platter, alternate the ham and chicken in three long rows. Set aside in a warm oven.

Wash the broccoli thoroughly. Cut off only the tender tips and stems (about 3 inches long). In a pot, boil sufficient water to cover the broccoli. When boiling, add the soda, then put in the broccoli and stir for about 1 minute, remove from the stove, drain off the water and rinse the broccoli with cold water. This step is done to preserve the green color of the vegetable.

STEP 5:

In a preheated wok, add the vegetable oil, and when hot, quick-fry the broccoli for 1 minute. Then add the sugar, soy sauce, and wine, and stir evenly.

STEP 6:

Blend the cornstarch with 1½ cups of the reserved stock, and add to the vegetable mix. Turn off the heat. Arrange the broccoli stems as a border around the chicken/ham layers, and spoon the remaining liquid over the entire dish. Serve immediately.

Serves four.

Lemon Chicken
≈ Ning Mon Gai ≈

HAVE READY:
- 1 chicken breast, uncooked (remove skin and thin-slice into 4 pieces about ¼" x 5"; salt)
- 1 quart vegetable oil

HAVE READY FOR BATTER:
- ½ cup all-purpose flour
- ¼ cup cornstarch
- ½ teaspoon baking powder
- ¼ teaspoon salt
- ¾ cup water
- ½ teaspoon vegetable oil

STEP 1:
Stir ingredients for batter until the batter is smooth and the consistency of a ribbon stream.

STEP 2:
Heat 1 quart vegetable oil in a wide-based, deep-sided skillet until it is very hot (375° F.). Dip each piece of chicken into the batter and let the excess drip back into the batter bowl. Slip each piece into the hot oil, deep-frying one at a time. Allow about 5 minutes per piece. Be sure that the oil is hot for each piece of chicken so that it becomes crisp and not soggy. Remove, drain on paper toweling and set aside.

HAVE READY FOR LEMON SAUCE:
- 3 tablespoons fresh lemon juice
- 3 tablespoons sugar
- ½ cup water
- 1 teaspoon cornstarch blended with 2 tablespoon water
- a few drops of red food coloring

STEP 3:
Mix the water, lemon juice and sugar, pour into a wok and bring to a boil. Add the cornstarch blend and stir over heat until the mixture thickens.

Add the few drops of red food coloring, stir
and turn off the heat.

STEP 4:
Make a garnish of lemons cut into thin half-slices,
and maraschino cherries.

STEP 5:
To serve, arrange the 4 pieces of chicken in the
center of a platter. Cut each piece into 5 smaller
pieces, but retain the shape of the original piece.
Pour the hot lemon sauce over the chicken.
Arrange the half-slices of lemon around the
border of the platter, between the chicken pieces.
Place a cherry on each lemon slice. To maintain
crispness of the chicken, serve immediately.

Serves four.

Beggar's Chicken
🎌 Hut Yee Gai 🎌

(This recipe will take advance preparation in
assembling wrappings for the chicken. You will
need 2 pounds of ordinary low-fire wet clay
which usually can be bought in 25-pound bags
from a potter's shop or craft store. You will also
need 10 lotus leaves which are available in a
Chinatown grocery store. If unavailable, substitute
banana leaves. A third wrapping is aluminum
foil.)

PREPARE AHEAD:
1 1½–2 pound frying chicken, cleaned and dried

PREPARE MARINADE:

1 teaspoon salt	1 teaspoon light
1 teaspoon dark	Chinese soy sauce
Chinese soy sauce	1 teaspoon red
¼ teaspoon sesame oil	cooking wine
1 teaspoon sugar	

STEP 1:

Mix these ingredients together and brush on inside and outside of chicken. Marinate for 3 hours, occasionally brushing on more marinade outside, and rolling it around inside.

PREPARE STUFFING:

2 tablespoons thin-sliced Virginia ham
   (It is nearest in taste to Chinese ham.)
1 tablespoon sliced canned water chestnuts
1 tablespoon black mushrooms, thin-sliced, soaked 15 minutes, washed and drained

STEP 2:

Put stuffing into the chicken cavity, but don't sew it up. Place leaves on a tray so they overlap. Center chicken on the leaves, breast side up, then bring the leaves over the chicken, completely covering it. Wrap in two thicknesses of aluminum foil. Then take a handful of wet clay, flatten it out and start covering the foiled chicken, continuing until it is completely encased in the clay, but marking the outside to denote it is the breast-side. Bake in a pre-heated oven at 350° F. Place the chicken on a shallow baking dish, bake for 1½ hours, then raise to 400° F. and bake for another 1½ hours.

STEP 3:

To serve, place the clay-baked chicken on a wooden tray, breast-side up. Cover with a large dinner napkin and bring to the table. Show it to your guests, then recover with the napkin and with a judicious rap done by a wooden mallet, break the clay shell. Fold the foil back to make a rolled collar around the chicken, then peel back the leaves and pass the chicken around, allowing each guest to help himself. The chicken will be fork-tender.

Serves four.

(Note: If you use lotus leaves, soak them in water for 2 hours, drain, recover with water, and boil for 1 hour to remove the bitter taste. Drain water and set leaves aside until needed.)

China has had the largest population in the world for centuries, and most of those times were marked by a general struggle for existence, especially among the poorer classes. Forced to live from hand-to-mouth, they would beg or steal their food and prepare it as best they could.

If fortunate enough to steal a chicken, for instance, they would immediately dig a hole in the ground, wrap tree leaves and mud around the chicken, build a fire in the hole, place the mud-encased chicken on the coals and cover it to conserve fuel. A few hours later they would dig it up, break open the hardened clay shell, unwrap the leaves, and tear the chicken into pieces to be devoured on the spot.

While very unglamorous, from this basic procedure of keeping alive as best one could has come my recipe for Beggar's Chicken, now considered a gourmet dish throughout the world.

Chicken with Chinese Vegetables
☵ Ching Choy Gai ☵

HAVE READY:

5 tablespoons vegetable oil

1 cup whole Chinese black mushrooms, washed and soaked for 15 minutes

1 cup celery hearts, cut into 1-inch diagonal slices

1 cup Chinese cabbage, cut into 1-inch diagonal slices

water

1 teaspoon salt

1 teaspoon sugar

1 cup sliced bamboo shoots

1 cup sliced canned water chestnuts

1 cup canned button mushrooms

1 cup pea pods

1 ¼" slice of ginger root, or 1 clove mashed garlic

1 cup uncooked, boned white chicken meat cut into 2-inch strips

1 teaspoon light Chinese soy sauce

1 tablespoon dark Chinese soy sauce

1 teaspoon cornstarch

STEP 1:

Coat the bottom and sides of a preheated wok with 2 tablespoons vegetable oil. Add the black mushrooms, celery, cabbage, and ¼ cup water. Cover and quick-fry for 2 minutes. To this mixture add the salt and sugar, then the bamboo shoots, water chestnuts, canned mushrooms and pea pods. Cover and fry for 1 minute. Put in a bowl and set aside.

STEP 2:

Preheat the wok or skillet and coat bottom and sides with 1 tablespoon oil. Stir around the ginger or garlic, remove and discard. Add the chicken. (If this is your main dish, use 2 cups of chicken and quick-fry in 1 more tablespoon of oil.) Fry uncovered for 5 minutes, then add the soy sauces and stir.

STEP 3:

Combine the vegetable and chicken mixtures, add a blend of 1 teaspoon cornstarch and 1 teaspoon water, and mix well.

Serves four.

Cashew Chicken

🎘 Iu Kwo Chow Gai Ding 🎘

HAVE READY:

2 tablespoons vegetable oil	1 cup chicken broth
½ teaspoon salt	½ cup cooked cashew nuts
1 cup sliced chicken breast	½ teaspoon M.S.G. (optional)
½ cup pea pods	¼ teaspoon sugar
½ cup whole button mushrooms	½ teaspoon cornstarch
½ cup bamboo shoots	½ teaspoon water

STEP 1:

Preheat the wok and swirl 2 tablespoons of vegetable oil around the bottom and sides, sprinkle in salt and quick-fry the chicken for 2 minutes, then add pea pods, mushrooms, bamboo shoots and chicken broth, and cover and cook for 2 or 3 minutes.

STEP 2:

Gently stir in the cashew nuts, M.S.G., and sugar, and thicken with a pre-prepared paste of ½ teaspoon cornstarch with ½ teaspoon water. Serve immediately.

Serves four.

Duck & Other Fowl

Peking Duck
🔃 Buk King Kwa Lo Aap 🔃

(Please read this recipe carefully before you proceed. Peking Duck is one of the most famous of Chinese dishes, and if prepared properly, it is both a rare taste treat and a dinner-table conversation piece.)

HAVE READY:

1 freshly killed duck
(4½–5 pounds)
1 teaspoon salt
1 quart water
3 tablespoons honey
2 tablespoons cornstarch
blended with 4
tablespoons water

8 green onions with
stems
2 ¼" slices of ginger root
1 cylinder oven-ready
biscuits
1 small can plum sauce

PREPARE DUCK THE DAY BEFORE:

Clean the duck inside and out, and dry thoroughly. Salt lightly inside and out, and stuff with 2 green onions (with stems tied in a knot) and the ginger root. Bring the edges of the tail opening together and stitch with a length of fine wire. Attach another wire to the neck as a handle. Mix the water and honey in a large wok or small turkey roasting pan and bring to a boil. When boiling, stir in the cornstarch/water blend, and stir-boil to the consistency of a thin stream. Lower the heat. Holding the duck by the neck wire, dip into the liquid mixture three or four times to coat the duck completely on all sides.

Remove duck, hang overnight in a cool place, preferably with an electric fan to dry the skin thoroughly.

STEP 1:

In an oven preheated to 400° F., place the duck breast-up on a flat rack in the roasting pan. Roast 30 minutes, turn the duck over, lower the heat to 300° F. and roast 30 minutes more. Now

104

return the duck to breast-up position and roast for a final 30 minutes.

STEP 2:

Remove the oven-ready biscuits (such as Pillsbury's Butterfly Dinner Rolls) from the cylinder. Divide each biscuit in half. Bring 2 inches of water to boil in the bottom of a steamer, put the biscuits in the center part (above the water), cover and steam for 5 minutes.

STEP 3:

Thin-slice the stems of the remaining 6 onions into 2" diagonal strips. Put one-fourth of the strips on each butter plate with 1 teaspoon of plum sauce.

STEP 4:

Prepare the duck for serving by cutting off the drumsticks and wings, and placing them on a platter in the position the whole duck should be. Carefully slice off all skin pieces by about 1 inch by 2 inches and lay them aside. Slice the same pieces of meat from the bone. Place all the carved meat back on the platter, and cover with skin pieces on the outside to make it look like a whole duck.

To eat, split the biscuit in half. On one half, place the onion, plum sauce, duck and skin. Cover with the top and eat like a sandwich.

Serves four.

Eight Precious Duck

🔁 Bat Bow Aap 🔁

HAVE READY:

½ cup glutinous rice
3 cups water
½ cup chopped Virginia ham
½ cup cooked chestnuts, chopped
1 tablespoon chopped canned lotus seeds
2 tablespoons black mushrooms, washed, soaked overnight, tough stems cut away, then chopped
1 teaspoon canned chopped bamboo shoots

10 pieces small dried shrimp, cleaned and soaked in water for 2 hours, then rinsed
1 tablespoon canned chopped water chestnuts
1 4–5 pound duck, freshly killed
2 teaspoons salt
1 tablespoon dark Chinese soy sauce
1 teaspoon thin Chinese soy sauce
1 bunch Chinese parsley

1 red candied cherry

STEP 1:

Wash the glutinous rice and rinse several times to remove the excess starch. Put the rice in a pot, add the water, cover and bring to a boil over high heat. Uncover, and continue boiling until the rice is almost dry. Add the ham, chestnuts, lotus seeds, black mushrooms, bamboo shoots, dried shrimp and water chestnuts, and mix together. Cover and simmer over very low heat for about 15-20 minutes. Remove to a bowl, run a fork through to loosen mixture, and set aside to cool.

STEP 2:

Wash the duck thoroughly and remove the neck, giblets and any loose fat. Clean inside and out, then dry with paper towels. Rub the cavity with the salt, then spoon the cooled rice mixture into the tail cavity. Close up both the neck and tail openings with thread or skewers.

STEP 3:

Mix the soy sauces together on a flat plate and dip the duck in it, coating all sides. Place the duck breast-up on a rack in a roaster.

STEP 4:

Preheat the oven to 400° F., but turn it back to 350° before putting in the duck. Roast for 30 minutes, reduce the heat to 300° and turn the duck breast-down and roast for 20 minutes. Return to breast-up position for a final 15 to 20 minutes, or when it is golden brown.

STEP 5:

Remove to a platter rimmed with sprigs of Chinese parsley. Remove stitches or skewers from the openings, and place the candied cherry in the center of the duck, and serve.
Serves four.

(There are two ways to serve: the Chinese style is to set the platter on a lazy susan in the center of the table and invite each person to serve himself with chopsticks since the duck is so tender. For a continental manner of serving, cut the duck lengthwise, then in half, making four portions which can be eaten with a fork.)

Szechwan Duck
🔁 Cheun Char Aap 🔁

HAVE READY:

1 4-pound fresh duck water to cover	2 green onions with stems knotted around bulb
2 pieces star anise	
1 teaspoon Five-Spice powder	2 pieces of ginger root ¼" thick
2 tablespoons dark Chinese soy sauce	2 quarts vegetable oil
1 teaspoon peppercorns	2 cylinders oven-ready biscuits
4 teaspoons salt	

PREPARE DUCK THE DAY BEFORE:

Wash and clean the duck, cut off neck, remove gizzards and excess fat. To a pot of water sufficient to cover the duck, add the star anise, Five-Spice powder, soy sauce, ¾ teaspoon of the peppercorns, 1 teaspoon salt, onions and ginger root. Bring to a boiling stage, then add the duck, reduce to medium heat, and place the lid over two wooden chopsticks set across the pot to allow the steam to escape. Boil the duck for 2 hours.

Remove the duck to a bowl, and set aside to cool. When cooled, place in the refrigerator to chill overnight.

DEEP-FRY:

Just before cooking, take out the duck and dry it on paper toweling so that it will not spatter during the ensuing deep-frying period. Using a deep-fat-fryer large enough for the duck to lie flat, heat to 350° F. sufficient vegetable oil to cover the fowl. Place the duck on a wire mesh fryng basket and lower it by the handles into the oil. Deep-fry for 10 minutes. Reduce the flame to the lowest heat and simmer for 5 more minutes. If you are not using the wire basket, carefully lift the very tender duck out of the oil. Drain on paper towels. While it is cooling enough to permit you to remove the bones and cut into small serving pieces, prepare the rolls.

PREPARE ROLLS:

Heat water to boiling in the bottom of the steamer. Separate the rolls and place them on an oven-proof plate. When the water is boiling, place the plate inside the top section of the steamer, cover and steam for 5 minutes.

PREPARE PEPPER-SALT:

While the rolls are steaming, crush the remaining 1/4 teaspoon peppercorns, mix with salt and stir-fry for 2 or 3 minutes over low heat in your wok or skillet. Put in a small bowl and cool.

To serve, arrange the pieces of boned duck on a platter, the steamed rolls on another platter, and the Szechwan pepper-salt.

Serves four.

Pressed Almond Duck with Sweet & Sour Sauce

🔃 Teem Suen Baun Aap 🔃

HAVE READY:

1 4–5 pound fresh duck
    water to cover
	2 tablespoons dark
	    Chinese soy sauce

2 pieces star anise	1 teaspoon light Chinese soy sauce

2 green onions with
    stems tied around
    bulb
	1 teaspoon salt

1 1" piece ginger root,
    crushed
	2 tablespoons corn-
	    starch

	2 quarts vegetable oil

HAVE READY FOR SAUCE:

- ½ cup white vinegar
- 3 tablespoons catsup
- ¼ cup brown sugar
- 2 drops red food coloring
- 2 tablespoons corn- starch blended with 3 tablespoons water
- ¼ cup crushed toasted almonds

PREPARE DUCK THE DAY BEFORE:

Place the duck in a large pot and add water to cover. To the water, add the star anise, green onions, ginger root, soy sauces and salt. Cover and turn to high heat. Bring to a boil, turn to medium heat and cook for 2 hours until tender.

Remove the duck and allow to cool. Skin, debone and shred the duck meat. (If, like many Chinese, you enjoy the skin, leave some of it on as it will produce a crisper texture when deep-fried.)

Pack the shredded duck into a square cooking pan to a ¾" thickness. Sprinkle cornstarch generously over one side, then turn it over and do the same on the other side until completely coated. Heat water to boiling in the bottom of a steamer. Place the duck in the top section, cover and steam for 30 minutes. Remove and cool. Refrigerate overnight.

DEEP FRY:

On the next day, take the duck out of the refrigerator, cut into four quarters and drain each on paper toweling so there will be no moisture to splatter. In a deep-fryer, heat the 2 quarts of vegetable oil to 350° F. Add the duck quarters and deep-fry for 10 minutes, then remove with a slotted spoon and drain on paper towels. Cut into 1-inch squares and place on a serving platter.

PREPARE SAUCE:

While the duck is deep-frying, prepare the sweet and sour sauce. Mix together the vinegar, catsup, brown sugar, and red food coloring. Pour into a skillet and bring to a boil. Add the corn-

starch and water blend, and cook until the syrup
thickens to the desired consistency.
Pour the sauce over the duck, sprinkle with the
crushed almonds and serve immediately.

Serves four.

Champagne Pearl Duck
🔄 Heung Bun Aap 🔄

HAVE READY:

1 fresh duck, 3–4
    pounds
1 tablespoon salt
2 tablespoons dark
    Chinese soy sauce
1 tablespoon honey
3 quarts vegetable oil
1 cup champagne
½ cup chicken broth
2 cups water

12 pearl onions (wash,
    peel off tough
    outside skin, dry)
2 tablespoons corn-
    starch blended
    with 3 tablespoons
    water
1 bunch fresh Chinese
    or American parsley

STEP 1:
Wash and clean the duck inside and out. Rub
the cavity with the salt, then coat the outside
with a mixture of 1 tablespoon soy sauce and the
tablespoon of honey.

STEP 2:
In a roaster heat the vegetable oil to 350° F.
Add the duck and deep-fry on one side for
10 minutes, turn over and deep-fry for another
10 minutes so that it browns evenly. Remove
from the oil and set aside. Pour the oil into a
container to save for use at a later time.

STEP 3:
Wash and dry the roaster, and return the duck to
it. Make a blend of the wine (champagne), the
remaining soy sauce, chicken broth and water,
and pour over the duck. Place the roaster across

two burners on the stove top, cook over medium
heat until the liquid comes to a boil, then
reduce the heat to medium low and cook slowly
for 2 hours. Remove the duck to a serving
platter and set aside.

STEP 4:
Add the whole onions to the liquid and cook
several minutes until they are tender but still
retain their round shape. Alternate 1 sprig of
parsley and 1 onion around the rim of the duck
platter.

STEP 5:
Bring the liquid in the roaster to a boil, add the
cornstarch/water mixture and stir until the liquid
is thickened. Pour the hot sauce over the duck
and onions, and serve at once. It will be tender
enough to eat with chopsticks.

Serves four generously.

Egg Garnished Duck
🈁 Hom Dahn Hung Siu Aap 🈁

HAVE READY:

1 duck (2½ to 3 pounds)	1 teaspoon sugar
1 tablespoon salt	½ can chicken broth
¼ teaspoon pepper	2 cups water
2 tablespoons dark soy sauce	2 tablespoons corn- starch blended with 2 tablespoons water
1 tablespoon honey (optional)	6 hardboiled eggs
3 quarts vegetable oil	1 bunch fresh parsley
1 tablespoon cooking wine	

STEP 1:
Clean the duck carefully inside and out, and rub
with the salt, pepper and 1 tablespoon dark soy

sauce. If you prefer a sweet taste, rub on the honey. Now heat 3 quarts of oil in a roaster and when it is hot (about 350°) put in the duck and deep-fry for 10 minutes, turning it over so that it browns evenly, then remove from oil.

STEP 2:

Make a blend of the cooking wine, 1 tablespoon dark soy sauce, 1 teaspoon sugar, the chicken broth and 2 cups of water, and after you have removed the oil from the roaster, pour in this blend over the duck. Place the roaster on two burners on top of the stove, cook over medium heat until the liquid comes to a boil, then turn down flame to medium low and cook slowly for 2 hours. Remove the duck. Stir the cornstarch mixture into the roaster until it is thick (about 1 minute). Pour the hot mixture over the duck after you have placed it on an oval platter for serving.

Garnish the duck with slivers of the hardboiled eggs (6 from each egg, cut lengthwise), placing springs of parsley between the egg slivers.

Serves four.

Leftover Turkey with Oyster Sauce
⮔ Hao Yao Chow Foh Gai See ⮔

HAVE READY:

- 3 tablespoons vegetable oil
- 1 clove crushed garlic
- 1 large green pepper cut into 1 inch squares
- 1 medium sized white onion sliced into 1 inch pieces
- 3 cups left-over turkey,
- cut into 1 inch chunks
- 1 teaspoon light soy sauce
- 1 tablespoon dark soy sauce
- ½ teaspoon sugar
- 1 tablespoon oyster sauce

113

METHOD:

Preheat the wok or skillet over high heat. Add the oil. Swirl garlic around sides and bottom, and discard the garlic. Add the pepper and onion; stir for 1 minute. Add the turkey. Stir another minute. Add the soy sauces, sugar and oyster sauce, stir evenly and serve.

Serves four.

Minced Squab with Lettuce
🜋 Sang Choy Bak Kub Soong 🜋

HAVE READY:

- 3 tablespoons vegetable oil
- 2 slices ¼" thick ginger root
- 2 squab, boned, skinned and chopped (substitute can be Cornish game hens)
- ¼ cup black mushrooms, washed, soaked in warm water for 15 minutes, drained, with tough stems cut off, then chopped
- 1 teaspoon dark Chinese soy sauce
- ½ teaspoon salt
- ½ teaspoon sugar
- ¼ cup fresh or frozen tiny green peas
- ¼ cup canned chopped water chestnuts
- 1 tablespoon canned chopped bamboo shoots
- ¼ cup cooked chopped Virginia ham
- 1 teaspoon sesame oil
- 8 pieces of head lettuce (cut a small head in half, peel off the damaged outside leaves, then peel 8 good leaves, wash and set aside)

METHOD:

Preheat the wok, then add the vegetable oil over high heat. When hot, swirl the ginger slices around the bottom and sides of the wok, remove and discard the ginger. Add the chopped squab; stir-fry for about a minute. Add the mushrooms and stir-fry another minute. Now add the soy sauce, salt and sugar and stir-fry for a minute, then add the peas, water chestnuts and bamboo shoots, and stir together. Add the ham and mix evenly. Stir in the sesame oil and immediately remove from the wok to a serving platter. Put the lettuce leaves on another platter.

This dish is served as a first course, like an appetizer. Each person takes 1 lettuce leaf, then serves himself 2 tablespoons of the cooked squab, rolling it up in the leaf like a tortilla and eating it with the fingers.

Serves four.

Beef Dishes

Wu's Beef
🔁 Ng See Ngau Yoke 🔁

HAVE READY:

1 piece of filet mignon or flank steak (about 1 pound), gristle removed (thin-slice across the grain into strips 2" long, ½" wide, ¼" thick)

2 quarts vegetable oil

2 teaspoons cornstarch

1½ tablespoons dark soy sauce

2½ teaspoons light soy sauce

1 teaspoon Hoisin sauce

½ teaspoon red cooking wine

½ teaspoon sugar (optional)

pinch salt and pepper

⅓ package Chinese rice noodles

½ cup coarsely chopped onions

3 tablespoons water

1 teaspoon oyster sauce

STEP 1:
Marinate the beef for 15 minutes in a blend of 1 tablespoon each of vegetable oil, cornstarch and dark soy sauce, 2 teaspoons light soy sauce, 1 teaspoon Hoisin sauce, ½ teaspoon cooking wine, and a pinch of sugar, salt and pepper.

STEP 2:
In a deep fryer, bring the remaining vegetable oil (about 2 quarts) to 400° F. over high heat. (To test for readiness, drop in one strand of the rice noodles and if it pops up immediately, the oil is hot enough.) Put in the skein of noodles, and they will explode into a large puff upon contact with the oil. Take out immediately and set aside to drain on paper toweling.

STEP 3:
In a preheated wok or skillet, coat the sides and bottom over high heat with 2 tablespoons vegetable oil. Quick-fry the chopped onions for

118

1 minute, then add the marinated beef and cook
2 more minutes. (Stir very little or the meat will
become too watery.)

STEP 4:

Make a thickening of 3 tablespoons water, 1 teaspoon oyster sauce, 1 teaspoon cornstarch,
¼ teaspoon sugar, ½ teaspoon light soy sauce
and 1 teaspoon dark soy sauce. When smooth,
add to the beef and onion mixture, stirring for
1 minute. Remove from heat.

To serve, place the noodles on a platter and
spoon the beef mixture over them. Do not mix.

Serves four.

Steamed Beef
🔁 Jing Ngau Yoke 🔁

HAVE READY:

1 tablespoon dark Chinese soy sauce	1 tablespoon cornstarch blended with 2 tablespoons water
1 teaspoon light Chinese soy sauce	1 dash M.S.G.
1 teaspoon red cooking wine	2 cups ground round steak
¼ teaspoon sesame oil	3 tablespoons diced canned water chestnuts
½ teaspoon vegetable oil	

STEP 1:

Make a mixture of the soy sauces, cooking wine,
sesame and vegetable oils, the cornstarch blend
and M.S.G. Mix with the ground round, then
add the water chestnuts and mix again;

STEP 2:

Transfer the meat mixture to a glass pie plate and
flatten the meat smoothly against the bottom
and sides of the dish.

STEP 3:

To steam, put about 2 inches of hot water in the bottom of your steamer, cover and bring to a boil. At the boiling point, place the pie plate mixture in the midsection of the steamer and cover. Steam for 10 minutes over high heat. Remove and serve immediately.

Serves four.

Beef with Green Pepper
⇄ Ching Jeu Chow Ngau Yoke ⇄

HAVE READY:

1 cup thin-sliced flank steak (about ½ pound)	(or substitute fresh mushrooms)
4½ tablespoons vegetable oil	¼ cup pea pods, sliced
½ teaspoon light soy sauce	2 bell peppers, thin-sliced
1 tablespoon dark soy sauce	2 green onions, thin-sliced
1 teaspoon cornstarch	2 hot chili peppers (red or green), thin-sliced
¼ cup thin-sliced black mushrooms, soaked overnight	½ teaspoon salt
	3 tablespoons chicken broth

1 teaspoon hot sauce

STEP 1:

Marinate the beef for a few minutes with 1 teaspoon vegetable oil, ½ teaspoon light soy sauce, 1 tablespoon dark soy sauce and 1 teaspoon cornstarch. Blend well. Set aside.

STEP 2:

Preheat the wok and swirl around 2 tablespoons vegetable oil, then stir-fry the black mushrooms for 1 minute. Now put in the pea pods, peppers and onions, stirring for 2 minutes. Finally add the hot peppers, salt, chicken broth and hot

120

sauce, and stir for 1 minute more. Put this mixture aside in a bowl.

STEP 3:

Heat the wok with 2 tablespoons vegetable oil, and when hot, put in the beef marinade. Stir-fry for 2 minutes, then add the vegetable mixture, stir and serve hot.

Serves four.

Beef Pepper Steak
⚘ See Jeu Ngau Yoke ⚘

HAVE READY:

1 **pound top sirloin steak, cut into 1″ pieces**	1 **teaspoon cornstarch**
5 **tablespoons vegetable oil**	1 **cup green pepper, cut into 1″ chunks**
1 **teaspoon oyster sauce**	½ **cup white onion, cut into 1″ pieces**
1 **teaspoon light soy sauce**	1 **tablespoon water**
1 **teaspoon dark soy sauce**	½ **teaspoon salt**
½ **teaspoon sugar**	1 **clove crushed garlic**
1 **teaspoon dry sherry**	¼ **teaspoon monosodium glutamate (optional)**

STEP 1:

Marinate the beef for 30 minutes in 1 tablespoon oil, the oyster sauce, soy sauces, sugar, sherry and cornstarch.

STEP 2:

Preheat the wok, then heat 2 tablespoons oil. When hot, add the pepper and onion, and quick-fry for 1 minute. Add 1 tablespoon water, ½ teaspoon salt and the monosodium glutamate. Stir 1 minute, then put into a bowl and set aside.

121

Wash, clean and dry the wok. Preheat, then heat 2 tablespoons oil. Swirl the garlic clove around the bottom and sides and discard. Add the marinated beef. Quick-fry on all surfaces for about 2 minutes. Do not stir too much or the meat will become watery. When dark brown, add the vegetable mixture, stir in thoroughly and serve immediately.

Serves four.

Beef & Asparagus with Black Bean Sauce
🔁 Ngau Yoke Dow See Chow Lo Suhn 🔁

HAVE READY:

2 cups beef, cut across the grain into 2" by 1" by ¼" strips	¼ cup black Chinese beans
1 tablespoon dark Chinese soy sauce	2 cups uncooked asparagus (only the tender stalks— cut into 1½" diagonal slices)
1 teaspoon light Chinese soy sauce	
4 tablespoons vegetable oil	2 cloves garlic
1 teaspoon salt	1½ teaspoons water
⅛ teaspoon sugar	¼ teaspoon monosodium glutamate
	1 ¼" slice ginger root

STEP 1: (MARINATE OVERNIGHT)
Marinate the beef strips in the soy sauces, 1 tablespoon vegetable oil, ⅛ teaspoon salt and ⅛ teaspoon sugar for 10 minutes. If possible, marinate overnight.

STEP 2:
Wash the black beans thoroughly and put into a small bowl. Peel the garlic cloves and add them to the black beans, mashing into a smooth blend.

STEP 3:
   Preheat the wok and coat bottom and sides with 2 tablespoons vegetable oil. Add the mashed beans and asparagus slices. Stir well and quick-fry for 3 minutes. Add ½ teaspoon salt, 1½ teaspoons water and ¼ teaspoon monosodium glutamate, blend well, cover and cook over medium heat for 5 minutes. Set aside.

STEP 4:
   Preheat wok and coat bottom and sides with 1 tablespoon oil. Add the ginger slice, coating bottom and sides, then discard the ginger. Stir in the marinated beef and turn with a spatula to brown evenly. When browned, add the cooked asparagus mixture, stirring well. Serve hot.

   Serves four.

Beef Lo Mein with Oyster Sauce
🔁 Hao Yao Ngau Yoke Lo Mein 🔁

HAVE READY:
   1 pound egg noodles
   4 tablespoons vegetable oil
   1 piece (about 1 pound) flank steak, with gristle removed (thin-slice across the grain into 2″ by ¼″ strips)

FOR MARINADE:
   1 tablespoon vegetable oil
   1 teaspoon cornstarch
   1 tablespoon dark Chinese soy sauce
   ½ teaspoon red cooking wine
   1 pinch sugar (optional)
   1 pinch salt and pepper

STEP 1:
   Break the noodles in half and drop into a pot of boiling water. Cover and cook at high heat for 15 minutes. Do not overcook. Put noodles in

a colander and rinse thoroughly under the cold water faucet. Put in a bowl and add 1 tablespoon vegetable oil to keep the noodles from sticking together. Set aside.

STEP 2:

Marinate the beef for a minimum of 5 minutes in the mixture of 1 tablespoon vegetable oil, the cornstarch, dark soy sauce, wine, and a pinch of sugar, salt and pepper.

HAVE READY:

marinated beef (as done above)
1 tablespoon vegetable oil
2 cloves garlic, crushed
1 teaspoon light Chinese soy sauce
2 tablespoons oyster sauce

½ teaspoon sugar
1 cup fresh pea pods, sliced
1 cup sliced canned water chestnuts
2 teaspoons cornstarch blended with ⅓ cup water

STEP 3:

In a preheated wok, over high heat coat the bottom and sides with vegetable oil. Rub the garlic over the sides and bottom, then discard the garlic.

Quick-fry the beef, stirring with a spatula to brown all sides uniformly. When brown, add the pea pods and water chestnuts, then the soy sauce, oyster sauce and sugar, stirring well.

Thicken the mixture with the cornstarch and water blend. Make a bed of noodles on a platter and spoon the beef over them.

Serves four.

Beef Tomato
🔃 Fan Ken Ngau Yoke 🔃

HAVE READY:
  2 cups flank steak (about 1 pound), gristle and fat
      removed (slice in half across the grain lengthwise
      into strips 1½" long, 1" wide, ¼" thick)

FOR MARINADE:
  1 tablespoon vegetable oil
  1 teaspoon light Chinese soy sauce
  1 tablespoon dark Chinese soy sauce
  1 teaspoon cornstarch
  ½ teaspoon cooking wine

FOR SAUCE:

1 tablespoon vegetable oil	removed, coarsely chopped (optional)
1 medium sized yellow onion, coarsely chopped (optional)	2 cups fresh tomatoes, ⅛ wedges cut in half
1 cup green peppers, seeds and pulp	1 teaspoon salt
	¼ teaspoon sugar
½ cup catsup	

STEP 1:
  Marinate the beef for 15 minutes in a mixture
  of 1 tablespoon vegetable oil, the soy sauce,
  cornstarch and wine.

STEP 2:
  In a preheated wok or skillet, over high heat,
  coat sides and bottom with oil. Quick-fry the
  onions. Add the peppers, cook 1 minute. Then
  add the tomatoes, salt and sugar, stir for 3 minutes, cover and cook for 1 minute more. Add
  the catsup, stir and pour mixture into a bowl.
  Set aside.

125

HAVE READY:

- 1 tablespoon vegetable oil
- 1 clove crushed garlic
- 2 cups marinated beef strips (done above)
- 1 teaspoon cornstarch blended with
    2 tablespoons water
- ½ teaspoon salt

STEP 3:

Clean the wok, preheat and coat sides and bottom with the oil. Rub on garlic clove, remove and discard garlic. Add the marinated beef (done above), turning over to brown uniformly. Now add the vegetable mixture and stir over high heat. Make a well in the center, pour in the blended cornstarch, add salt and stir to thicken. Serve immediately.

Serves four.

Beef Bean Curd with Oyster Sauce

🔁 Hao Yao Dow Fu Ngau Yoke 🔁

FOR MARINADE:

- 1 cup thin-sliced flank or Spencer steak, sliced into pieces ½" thick, 1" wide and 2½" long
- 1 tablespoon vegetable oil
- 1 teaspoon light Chinese soy sauce
- 1 tablespoon dark Chinese soy sauce
- 1 teaspoon cornstarch
- ¼ teaspoon sugar
- 1 teaspoon red cooking wine

STEP 1:

Mix marinade in a bowl, add meat and set aside. It is ready for use.

FOR QUICK-FRY:
   3 squares bean curd about 3" x 3" x 1", cut
      into strips about ¼" wide
   1 green onion with 6 inches of stem, thin-sliced
      into 2" lengths (makes 18 strips)
   2 tablespoons vegetable oil

FOR SAUCE:
   2 tablespoons oyster sauce
   ½ teaspoon sugar
   1 tablespoon water
   ½ teaspoon cornstarch
   1 teaspoon dark Chinese soy sauce
   ¼ teaspoon M.S.G. (optional)

STEP 2:
Blend together and set aside.

STEP 3:
Add 2 tablespoons vegetable oil to a preheated
wok or skillet. When hot, add the onions, stir
and immediately add the marinated meat, then
quick-fry about 2 minutes. Add the bean curd
strips (but be careful not to mash them—use a
spatula). Quick-fry another minute or two.

Add the oyster sauce, blend, mix well, remove
to a platter and serve hot.

Serves four.

Stuffed Squash
🈂 Yeun Jit Kwa 🈂

HAVE READY:

- 2 Chinese squash about 6" long and 2½" in diameter (wash, cut off about 1" from stem end, hollow out seeds and center, and discard seeds and center
- 3 tablespoons vegetable oil
- 1 teaspoon light Chinese soy sauce
- 5 teaspoons dark Chinese soy sauce
- ½ teaspoon cornstarch dash salt and pepper
- ½ pound ground sirloin
- ¼ cup water chestnuts, chopped fine
- ¼ cup mushrooms, chopped fine
- 1 teaspoon sugar
- 1 tablespoon water pinch M.S.G.
- ½ teaspoon sesame oil

STEP 1:

Prepare a marinade of 1 teaspoon vegetable oil, 1 teaspoon light soy sauce, 1 teaspoon dark soy sauce, ½ teaspoon cornstarch and dash of salt and pepper. Mix with the ground sirloin, then stir in the water chestnuts and mushrooms. Marinate for 10 minutes, then stuff into squash and attach hollowed-out tops with toothpicks.

STEP 2:

Place squash on a plate and set in the middle section of a steamer. Steam over 2 inches of boiling water (it must not touch the squash) for 30 minutes, covered.

STEP 3:

Heat 1 tablespoon oil in preheated wok, and put in the squash. Mix together 2 tablespoons dark soy sauce, 1 teaspoon sugar, 1 tablespoon water, dash of M.S.G. and ½ teaspoon sesame oil and pour over squash. Now turn over the squash and spoon over more sauce.

Remove the squash to a platter, slice into ¾ inch
pieces, and spoon on any sauce remaining in
the wok. Serve hot immediately.

Serves four.

Beef with Oyster Sauce
🔃 Hao Yao Ngau Yoke 🔃

HAVE READY:

3 teaspoons vegetable
oil
1 ½" piece ginger
root or garlic
clove
1½ cups tenderloin
steak (about ¾
pound), cut across
the grain into
2" by ½" by ¼"
strips
½ cup sliced bamboo
shoots

½ cup sliced button
mushrooms
1 cup snow peas
½ cup chicken broth
4 teaspoons oyster
sauce
½ teaspoon dark soy
sauce
¼ teaspoon sesame oil
¼ teaspoon sugar
½ teaspoon cornstarch
blended with
½ teaspoon water

METHOD:

Swirl the vegetable oil in a preheated wok, then
add ginger or garlic, stirring to add flavor to
the oil. Discard ginger or garlic. Quick-fry the
tenderloin pieces for about 2 minutes, then add
the bamboo shoots, mushrooms, pea pods and
chicken broth. Cover for 1 minute.

Now uncover, and stir in the oyster sauce, the
soy sauce, sesame oil and sugar, and thicken with
the cornstarch blend. Serve immediately.

Serves four.

Beef with Pea Pods & Water Chestnuts
🐉 Ngau Yoke Ma Tai Chow Ho Lan Dow 🐉

HAVE READY:

1 pound flank steak, with gristle removed (thin-slice across the grain into 2" by 1" strips)

5 tablespoons vegetable oil

1 teaspoon cornstarch

1 tablespoon dark soy sauce

2 teaspoons light soy sauce

½ teaspoon red cooking wine

½ teaspoon sugar (optional)

1¼ teaspoon salt

1 pound Chinese pea pods

½ cup canned sliced water chestnuts

¼ cup canned sliced bamboo shoots

½ teaspoon monosodium glutamate

1 clove crushed garlic

STEP 1:
Marinate the beef for 30 minutes in a mixture of 1 tablespoon oil, cornstarch, the soy sauces, wine, sugar and ¼ teaspoon salt.

STEP 2:
Pull strings off both ends of the pea pods, wash and dry thoroughly on paper towels.

STEP 3:
In a preheated wok, heat 2 tablespoons oil. Quick-fry the pea pods for 1 minute. Add the water chestnuts and bamboo shoots, and mix well for 1 minute. Add 1 teaspoon salt, the monosodium glutamate and stir. Remove to a bowl with a slotted spoon, leaving the excess liquid in the wok. Discard liquid.

STEP 4:
Wash, clean and dry wok. Preheat, then heat 2 tablespoons oil. Swirl garlic clove around top and sides, then discard clove. Add the marinated beef, quick-fry on both sides, turning each piece

separately for about 2 minutes. Blend in the cooked pea pod mixture and serve immediately.

Serves four.

Bitter Melon & Beef with Black Bean & Garlic Sauce

🔃 See Chup Fu Kwa Ngau Yoke 🔃

HAVE READY:

2 cups flank steak (about 1 pound), fat and gristle removed (cut steak in half lengthwise, then thin-slice across the grain)	1 teaspoon dry sherry
	2 teaspoons sugar
	1 cup bitter melon water
4 tablespoons vegetable oil	2 tablespoons canned black bean sauce, mixed with
2 tablespoons dark Chinese soy sauce	2 cloves crushed garlic
1 tablespoon cornstarch	¼ teaspoon salt
	¼ teaspoon monosodium glutamate (optional)

STEP 1:

Marinate the beef for a few minutes in 1 tablespoon vegetable oil, the soy sauce, cornstarch, sherry and 1 teaspoon of sugar. Set aside.

STEP 2:

Slice off both ends of the bitter melon, then cut in half lengthwise and scoop out the pulp and seeds. Thin-slice. Bring water to boil in a pot, and when it is boiling, turn off the heat and submerge the melon slices. Let them blanch for 1 minute, then discard the water and drain the melon on paper towels. (Blanching removes the bitter taste of the melon.) Set aside.

131

STEP 3:
Preheat the wok and add the remaining 3 tablespoons of vegetable oil. When hot, add the mixture of bean sauce and garlic, stir for several seconds, and add the beef strips, being careful not to stir too much or the beef will get watery.

Stir-fry for 1 or 2 minutes until the separated pieces of beef are brown on both sides. Add the bitter melon, salt, the remaining teaspoon of sugar, and the monosodium glutamate. Stir evenly, remove from the fire and serve hot.

Serves four.

Beef with Cauliflower
🔃 Yea Choy Far Chow Ngau Yoke 🔃

HAVE READY:

3 tablespoons vegetable oil	1 ¼" slice fresh ginger root
1 head cauliflower, cut into flowerets 3 inches long	1 cup flank steak, cut into 1" by 2" strips
¼ teaspoon salt	1 teaspoon dark soy sauce
3 tablespoons water	1 teaspoon oyster sauce
½ teaspoon sugar	
¼ teaspoon M.S.G. (optional)	

STEP 1:
Swirl 2 tablespoons oil around bottom and sides of a preheated wok or skillet, then add the cauliflower, stir for 1 minute, cover, continue cooking over high heat for 5 minutes. Stir in the salt, water, ¼ teaspoon sugar and M.S.G., then lower to medium heat and cook another 5 minutes. Now set aside.

STEP 2:

In another preheated wok or skillet, swirl around 1 tablespoon oil, stir-fry the ginger slice to flavor the oil, then remove and discard the ginger. Quick-fry ½ cup of the beef at a time to insure uniform browning. Stir in the soy sauce, oyster sauce and ¼ teaspoon sugar.

Drain the liquid from the cooked cauliflower, and stir the flowerets into the browned meat. Remove and serve hot.

Serves four.

Ginger Beef
🜨 Gee Kuen Ngau Yoke 🜨

(This dish should be made only with fresh ginger, which is available in Chinese markets from April to October.)

HAVE READY:

2 cups flank steak (about 1 pound), fat and gristle removed (cut steak in half lengthwise, then thin-slice across the grain)	2 tablespoons dark Chinese soy sauce
	1 teaspoon thin Chinese soy sauce
	1 teaspoon dry sherry
2 teaspoons cornstarch	1 teaspoon sugar
4 tablespoons vegetable oil	½ cup fresh ginger, pared and thin-sliced
	¼ teaspoon salt

STEP 1:

Marinate the meat for a few minutes with a mixture of the cornstarch, 1 tablespoon vegetable oil, the soy sauces, sherry and sugar. Set aside.

STEP 2:

Preheat the wok and add 1 tablespoon of oil. When hot, add the ginger, stir-fry for about

133

30 seconds over medium heat. Add the salt, stir-fry another 30 seconds. Drain off liquid, remove the ginger to a bowl and set aside.

STEP 3:

Wash, dry and preheat the wok. Turn to high heat, and add 2 tablespoons oil. When hot, add the marinated beef, separate each piece, and fry until brown on both sides (1 or 2 minutes). Add the ginger (from Step 2), stir evenly and serve immediately on a platter.

Serves four.

Pork Dishes

SUDDENLY NO SERVANTS

When I was in India, visiting friends on a houseboat in Kashmir, we had a visitor who came from Calcutta and brought with him several jars of shredded pork and shredded beef, which are usually eaten with a Chinese porridge or sprinkled lightly over an entree.

Behind our large vessel was a smaller boat in which the servants lived, and during tea, when the various dishes were being served, suddenly most of the servants rushed to the rail and jumped overboard.

At first our host was confused and embarrassed, and he called down to the men in the water to ask why they had abandoned the houseboat.

For a time no one would reply, but at last one of them spoke and explained that they were Moslems who never ate pork and had jumped into the river to cleanse themselves of the stain of having served it.

Furthermore, they refused to return until our Chinese chef and his assistants cleared away and washed the dishes, as well as discarding the pork.

Such a problem never arises in Chinese cooking, where there are no taboos. A Chinese dinner is a blend of all available ingredients and everything is used, from the chicken feet and head to the part that went over the fence last.

In vegetables, nothing is wasted: the roots, the stem, the main portion of the plant, and the leaves all find their way into a Chinese cooking pot.

Pork Bean Curd with Sauce
🔃 Dow Fu Geu Chu Yoke 🔃

HAVE READY:

4 bean curd squares
½ pound lean ground pork
4 shrimp (16 to a pound), chopped
¼ cup water chestnuts
¼ teaspoon salt
1 teaspoon light soy sauce

2 tablespoons dark soy sauce
1 teaspoon sugar (optional)
1 teaspoon wine
1 tablespoon cornstarch
¼ teaspoon sesame oil
1 egg, beaten slightly
1 quart vegetable oil

STEP 1:

Cut the bean curd squares into 4 triangular parts and hollow out the centers of each.

STEP 2:

Place the ground pork in a bowl, add the shrimp and water chestnuts, then marinate with the salt, soy sauces, sugar, wine, cornstarch and sesame oil. Stuff about 1 teaspoon of the well-blended marinade into the bean curd hollows, then dip this edge into the beaten egg to seal.

STEP 3:

Heat 1 quart oil in the wok to about 350° F., then drop in the bean curd sections a few at a time, deep-frying until toast brown, or until they float. Drain on paper toweling.

SAUCE FOR PORK BEAN CURD

HAVE READY:

1 tablespoon vegetable oil
2 green onions, thin-sliced or diced leftover pork (used for bean curd hollows)

2 tablespoons dark soy sauce
1 teaspoon chili paste with garlic
1 teaspoon Hoisin sauce
¾ cup chicken broth
¼ teaspoon sesame oil

METHOD:

Swirl around 1 tablespoon oil in the preheated wok, then stir-fry the green onions and leftover pork for 5 minutes. Add the soy sauce, chili paste, Hoisin sauce, chicken broth and sesame oil; stir in well. Now put in the bean curd triangles, stir thoroughly and serve hot.

Serves four.

Bean Curd with Pork Szechwan Style
🔃 Ma Po Dow Fu 🔃

HAVE READY:

2 tablespoons dark soy sauce	chopped green or white onion
1 tablespoon light soy sauce	1 tablespoon vegetable oil
1 tablespoon Hoisin sauce (optional)	8 ounces ground pork
1 teaspoon hot sauce (or tabasco sauce)	½ cup diced green pepper
2 tablespoons cornstarch	2 tablespoons Szechwan mustard pickles, washed in hot water (optional)
¼ teaspoon sesame oil	
2 tablespoons	4 pieces bean curd

STEP 1:

Mix the soy sauces, Hoisin sauce, hot sauce, cornstarch and sesame oil with the pork.

STEP 2:

Quick-fry the onion in 1 tablespoon vegetable oil, then add the pork mixture, green pepper, mustard pickles and bean curd, which you chop into sections as you are cooking. Stir-fry for 10 minutes, or until you are sure that the pork is done. Add more hot sauce to taste, if desired.

Serves four.

Sweet & Sour Pork
🔁 Ku Lo Yoke 🔁

HAVE READY:

½ cup all-purpose flour	¾ cup water
¼ cup cornstarch	2 quarts vegetable oil
¼ teaspoon baking powder	1 pound lean pork butt, cut into 1" squares
¼ teaspoon salt	

STEP 1:

Mix flour, cornstarch, baking powder, salt and water in a bowl and stir until the batter is the consistency of a smooth, thin stream.

STEP 2:

Heat the vegetable oil in a kettle until it is very hot (375° F.). Dip the pork chunks into the batter, allow excess to drip off, and gently drop them into the hot oil. Deep-fry for 12 minutes, then reduce heat to medium and deep-fry for an additional 10 minutes. Drain on paper towel.

SWEET & SOUR SAUCE

HAVE READY:

¾ cup catsup	1 cup green pepper chunks
¼ cup white vinegar	
1 cup juice from canned pineapple	1 tablespoon cornstarch blended with 3 tablespoons water
3 tablespoons sugar	
½ cup white onion slices	1 cup canned pineapple chunks

METHOD:

In a bowl, blend the catsup, vinegar, pineapple juice and sugar. Pour the mixture into a preheated wok or large skillet and bring to a boil over high heat. Add the onions and pepper, stirring over high heat, uncovered, for 3 minutes.

When at the boiling stage, add the cornstarch blend, return to a boil. Add the pineapple and the deep-fried pork chunks, stir well and serve immediately.

Serves four, generously.

Shanghai Year Rice Noodles
🔁 Sheung Hoi Nin Gou 🔁

(Ovaletts [chow nee gow] is another ingredient which has recently appeared in Chinese, Japanese and Korean markets. It is called "Year Rice" because it is a feature of the Chinese New Year's celebration.)

HAVE READY:

water
1 cup rice Ovaletts
4 tablespoons vegetable oil
1/3 cup black mushrooms, soaked in hot water for 15 minutes, drained and thin-sliced
3 cups white shredded celery cabbage
2 tablespoons chicken broth
1 teaspoon salt

2 green onions with 6" of stem, diagonally sliced
1/2 cup thin-sliced boiled ham or barbecued pork
1 teaspoon light soy sauce
2 teaspoons dark soy sauce
1 teaspoon sugar
1/4 teaspoon monosodium glutamate (optional)

STEP 1:
Heat sufficient water to cover Ovaletts. When boiling, drop them in and boil for 3 minutes. Remove and dry thoroughly on paper toweling.

STEP 2:
Heat sufficient water to cover Ovaletts. When hot, add mushrooms and stir, then add the cabbage, broth and salt, and stir-fry for about 3 minutes. With a slotted spoon, remove to a bowl, leaving the excess liquid in the wok.

Discard the liquid, wash and dry wok. Preheat it and add 2 tablespoons of oil. When hot, add the onions and ham, stir in the Ovaletts, and mix thoroughly. Now add the soy sauces, sugar and monosodium glutamate, and stir to blend. Add the cabbage mixture, stir thoroughly and serve immediately.

Serves four.

Lion's Head in Earth Pot
↻ Sar Woh See Gee Tao ↻

HAVE READY:

2 cups lean ground pork	1 tablespoon dark Chinese soy sauce
4 teaspoons cornstarch	1 teaspoon light Chinese soy sauce
½ teaspoon salt	1 egg
¼ teaspoon sugar	
1 quart vegetable oil	

STEP 1:

Mix all the above ingredients (except the vegetable oil) and roll into 4 balls. Heat the vegetable oil in a kettle to 375° F. and deep-fry the meat balls just long enough for them to turn light brown. Drain on paper toweling.

HAVE READY:

3 tablespoons vegetable oil	½ teaspoon sugar
1 head Chinese cabbage	¼ cup water
1½ teaspoons dark Chinese soy sauce	1 teaspoon cornstarch blended with 2 tablespoons water
1 teaspoon light Chinese soy sauce	

STEP 2:

Coat a preheated wok with 3 tablespoons oil. Slice off bottom of cabbage, cut head into half

141

and then slice lengthwise into fourths. Mix with soy sauces, salt, ½ teaspoon sugar and ¼ cup water, cover and cook over high heat for 15 minutes.

STEP 3:

Add the meatballs, placing them on top of the cabbage and do not stir. Cover and cook over medium heat for 30 minutes.

When serving, spoon out the cabbage leaves onto a platter as a bed for the meat balls. With the liquid left in the wok, add the cornstarch blend with ½ teaspoon sugar, stirring to thicken smoothly.

Pour this gravy over the meat balls to give them a shiny look. Serve hot.

Serves four.

Deep Fried Bean Curd with Pork Szechwan Style

🔃 Dow Fu Geu Chu Yoke 🔃

HAVE READY:

1 cup ground pork
1 teaspoon water
3 tablespoons vegetable oil
2 tablespoons dark soy sauce
2 teaspoons light soy sauce
1 teaspoon cornstarch
1 ½" slice ginger root

3 squares fresh bean curd (about 3" x 3" x 1"), cut into 1" squares
1 teaspoon chili paste with garlic
½ teaspoon sugar
¼ teaspoon mono-sodium glutamate (optional)

STEP 1:

Marinate the pork for a few minutes with 1 teaspoon water, 1 tablespoon dark soy sauce, 2 teaspoons light soy sauce, 1 teaspoon cornstarch and 1 tablespoon oil. Set aside.

Preheat the wok and heat 2 tablespoons oil.
When hot, swirl the ginger slice over the bottom
and sides, then discard the ginger. Add the
marinated pork, cook 4 to 5 minutes to be sure
the pork is done. Then add the bean curd squares
and press them down gently as you stir. Add
1 tablespoon dark soy sauce, the chili paste,
sugar and monosodium glutamate. Stir in well
and serve immediately.

Serves four.

Steamed Pork with Chinese Sausage
🔁 Lap Cheon Jing Chu Yoke 🔁

HAVE READY:

½ teaspoon light Chinese soy sauce	hour in cold water to remove excess salt and hot pepper, then thin-slice
1 teaspoon dark Chinese soy sauce	
1 teaspoon cooking sherry	2 tablespoons water
¼ teaspoon sugar	1 pound ground lean pork
1 tablespoon cornstarch	
¼ cup canned Chinese mustard pickles (soak well for an	2 links Chinese sausage
	1 tablespoon chopped green onion with stem

STEP 1:
In a bowl, combine the soy sauces, sherry, sugar,
cornstarch and water, and pickle slices. Add the
ground pork and mix thoroughly. Pat this mixture
into the bottom and sides of an oven-proof
shallow bowl which will fit into the top of your
steamer. Thin-slice the sausages and place them
in spoke fashion on top of the pork.

STEP 2:
Heat water in the bottom of the steamer. When
it is boiling, place the bowl in the top section
and cover with a lid. Steam for 20 minutes.

Before serving sprinkle the chopped onion over the top.

Serves four.

(This is one of my husband's favorite dishes.)

Three Flower Dish
🔁 Chow Sam Far 🔁

HAVE READY:

- 2 large pieces pork kidney soaked in salt water
- 2 tablespoons wine or whiskey
- 1 pork tripe
- 6 pieces chicken gizzards
- 5 tablespoons vegetable oil
- ¼ cup celery hearts, cut diagonally into 1″ lengths
- ¼ cup thin-sliced white onion
- ¼ cup Cloud Ear, presoaked and sliced
- ¼ cup canned sliced bamboo shoots
- ¼ teaspoon salt dash pepper
- 2 ¼″ thick slices ginger
- 2 cloves crushed garlic
- ½ teaspoon light soy sauce
- 1 tablespoon dark soy sauce
- ½ teaspoon sugar
- ½ teaspoon cornstarch blended with 1 tablespoon water
- ½ teaspoon sesame oil

STEP 1:

Clean kidneys in salt water. Drain and slice into pieces ½″ by 1″ by 2″. Discard remainder. Soak in 1 cup water and 1 tablespoon strong wine or whiskey for 30 minutes. Drain. Score surfaces diagonally to make a crisscross pattern, first crosswise, then lengthwise, about three-fourths of the depth of them.

Dip the tripe in boiling water and take out immediately. Soak in salted cold water for 30 minutes. Drain. Cut away all but thick portion.

144

Remove the skin, slice into ½″ thickness, 1″ wide and 2″ long. Score as you did the kidneys.

Wash, clean and drain the chicken gizzards. Remove the dark section. Thin-slice into ¼″ thick pieces and cut slits about ½″ long.

STEP 2:
Heat 2 tablespoons vegetable oil in a preheated wok. Add the celery, onion and Cloud Ear; quick-fry for 1 minute. Add the bamboo shoots, salt and pepper, stir, remove and set aside.

STEP 3:
Clean the wok, preheat and add 3 tablespoons vegetable oil. Coat bottom and sides with ginger and garlic, remove and discard the ginger and garlic. When oil is hot, add the kidney, tripe and gizzard, and quick-fry for about 2 minutes. Then stir in the vegetables, quick-fry for 1 minute more.

Now mix together the soy sauces, 1 teaspoon wine, ½ teaspoon sugar, a blend of ½ teaspoon cornstarch with 1 tablespoon water, and ½ teaspoon sesame oil. Add to the mixture, stir and serve hot.

Serves four.

Barbecued Pork with Vegetables
⚒ Char Sin Chow Ching Choy ⚒

HAVE READY:

3 tablespoons vege-
   table oil
1 ¼" slice ginger root
1 cup Chinese cabbage
   (use the tender
   center, wash
   thoroughly and
   cut into 2"
   lengths)
½ cup chicken broth
   (or water)
½ pound snow peas
   (pull strings)
½ cup canned whole
   button mushrooms
½ cup canned thin-
   sliced bamboo
   shoots

½ cup canned thin-
   sliced water
   chestnuts
2 teaspoons salt
¼ teaspoon mono-
   sodium glutamate
   (optional)
1 tablespoon thin-
   sliced green onion
   with stem
1 pound barbecued
   pork, thin-sliced
   (see page 29 for
   barbecued pork
   recipe)
1½ teaspoons cornstarch

STEP 1:

Add 2 tablespoons of oil to a preheated wok
over high heat. Swirl ginger root around bottom
and sides, then discard the ginger. Add Chinese
cabbage and stir-fry for 2 minutes, then add
¼ cup broth. Cover and cook for 1 minute.
Uncover and add the pea pods, mushrooms,
bamboo shoots, water chestnuts, salt and monosodium glutamate. Stir thoroughly for 1 minute.
Spoon into a bowl and set aside.

STEP 2:

Clean the wok, preheat and add 1 tablespoon of
oil. Add the thin-sliced onion and the barbecued
pork; stir-fry a few seconds. Add the vegetables
(from Step 1) and mix well. Blend the cornstarch
with the remaining ¼ cup of broth and stir
evenly into the mixture.

Using a slotted spoon so that the liquid remains in the wok, remove the pork and vegetables to a platter and serve immediately.

Serves four.

Sliced Pork with Green & Red Peppers
🔁 Lat Geu Chow Chu Yoke See 🔁

HAVE READY:

1 pound lean pork, thin-sliced into 2″ lengths	3 green onions with 4″ of stem, thin-sliced into 2″ lengths
1 tablespoon dark Chinese soy sauce	¼ teaspoon salt
1 teaspoon light Chinese soy sauce	1 cup thin-sliced green pepper
1 teaspoon red cooking wine	¼ cup thin-sliced small red pepper (remove inside seeds and veins)
1 tablespoon cornstarch	
4 tablespoons water	
¼ teaspoon sugar	
2 tablespoons vegetable oil	

STEP 1:
Marinate the pork with the soy sauces, wine, cornstarch, 2 tablespoons of water and the sugar.

STEP 2:
In a preheated wok, add the vegetable oil and swirl it around the bottom sides. Add the onion and then the pork; stir-fry for about 10 minutes. Add the salt and 2 tablespoons of water. Turn the heat down to low, cover and simmer for 10 minutes. Remove the cover, add the green and red pepper slices, and stir-fry for 2 minutes. Serve hot.

Serves four.

Spare Ribs with Black Bean Sauce

🔆 See Jeu Pai Kwat 🔆

HAVE READY:

- 1 1½ pound section of spare ribs (12 ribs)
- 4 large cloves garlic
- 1 ½" cube of ginger root
- 1 tablespoon vegetable oil
- 2 tablespoons black soybeans
- 3 tablespoons dark soy sauce (for color)
- 1 tablespoon light soy sauce (for taste)
- ½ teaspoon salt
- 2 teaspoons sugar
- ¼ cup water

STEP 1:

Trim fat from both sides of the meat, then separate into 12 ribs. Chop each rib into 4 pieces or ask your friendly butcher to do it for you.

STEP 2:

Put the peeled garlic cloves and the ginger through a garlic press. Preheat wok or skillet and coat the bottom and sides with 1 tablespoon oil. Over high heat quick-fry the garlic and ginger, then stir in the soybeans for 1 minute.

STEP 3:

Add the ribs, stirring with a spatula to insure all-over browning. The beans absorb the vegetable oil and the fat, but if you have not removed enough fat from the ribs before cooking, drain off the excess. Brown for 10 minutes.

STEP 4:

Add the soy sauces, salt, sugar and water. Cover and reduce heat to medium for about 10 minutes. Then lower heat to a simmer and continue for another 10 minutes. Remove to a platter.

Serves four.

Vegetable Dishes

Chili Garlic Chinese Cabbage
🔁 Sueen Tao Lat Jeu Yeh Choy 🔁

HAVE READY:

1 celery cabbage
(about 1½ to
2 pounds)
2 tablespoons vege-
table oil
½ can chicken broth
2 tablespoons dark
soy sauce

1 teaspoon light
soy sauce
1 teaspoon chili garlic
sauce
1 teaspoon sugar
¼ teaspoon mono-
sodium glutamate
(optional)

STEP 1:

Cut celery cabbage into quarters, then across
into 3 sections. Wash, drain and dry on paper
toweling. Preheat the wok and swirl around
2 tablespoons oil, then quick-fry the tougher
bottom parts of the cabbage. Now add the
chicken broth and the remainder of the cabbage,
and cook until soft, covered.

STEP 2:

Blend the soy sauces, the chili garlic sauce, sugar
and monosodium glutamate, and when the
cabbage is cooked, pour the mixture over it. If
you find that the blend is too thin, add a mixture
of 1 teaspoon cornstarch with 1 tablespoon water
and ¼ teaspoon sesame oil. Remove with a
slotted spoon and serve.

Serves four.

Chinese Mixed Green Vegetables
🔁 Sup Kum Ching Choy 🔁

HAVE READY:

2 cups Chinese
cabbage, chopped
2 tablespoons vege-
table oil
1 thin slice ginger root
1 clove crushed garlic
1 teaspoon salt
½ teaspoon sugar
¼ teaspoon mono-
sodium glutamate
(optional)
¼ cup chicken broth
½ cup pea pods
½ cup sliced bamboo
shoots
½ cup thin-sliced
mushrooms

METHOD:

Preheat wok and swirl around 2 tablespoons
vegetable oil, then rub buttom and sides with
the ginger root and garlic, and discard the ginger
and garlic. Put cabbage into the wok, stir, and
add the salt, sugar, monosodium glutamate and
chicken broth. Stir and cover; cook for
3 minutes. Now add the pea pods, bamboo
shoots, and mushrooms, stir for a half-minute,
then serve.

Serves four.

Broccoli with Straw Mushrooms
🔃 Choo Goo Chow Gai Lan Choy 🔃

HAVE READY:

1 pound broccoli
(Chinese or
American)

2 quarts water

1 teaspoon baking soda
(to preserve green
color)

3 tablespoons vege-
table oil

1 ginger root slice,
about ½"

1 8-ounce can straw
mushrooms (or
substitute canned

whole button
mushrooms)

½ teaspoon salt

½ teaspoon sugar

¼ teaspoon mono-
sodium glutamate
(optional)

1 can chicken broth

1 tablespoon cornstarch
blended with 2
tablespoons water
(can use chicken
stock instead of
water)

STEP 1:

Discard outer tough or wilted leaves from the
broccoli. Cut off and discard tough base end.
Take tender inside leaves, scrape away tough
fibers from the stems of the flowerets and cut
into 4" pieces. Wash.

STEP 2:

Bring water to a boil. Add the baking soda, then
the broccoli. Cover, bring to a boil and boil for
1 minute. Pour into a colander, rinse with cold
water, drain and dry on paper toweling. Set aside.

STEP 3:

In a preheated wok or skillet, add the oil and
swirl around the ginger slice, then discard the
ginger. Stir-fry the mushrooms for a few seconds,
the add the parboiled broccoli. Stir for 1 minute.
Now add the salt, sugar, monosodium glutamate
and broth, and stir for 1 minute. Stir in the
blended cornstarch and serve immediately.

Serves four.

Monk's Chicken
🔁 Chai Gai 🔁

(Usually included as part of the cold dishes in any Chinese gourmet dinner.)

HAVE READY:

5 semi-circular pieces of dried bean curd sheets (about half of a 9-ounce package)

⅔ cup chicken broth, with fat skimmed off

2 tablespoons dark soy sauce

2 teaspoons light soy sauce

2 teaspoons sesame oil

¼ teaspoon monosodium glutamate

½ tablespoon sugar

STEP 1:

Place one of the semi-circular dried bean curd sheets on a large cookie sheet. In a bowl, mix the broth, soy sauces, sesame oil, monosodium glutamate and sugar. Dip a 1" wide pastry brush into the liquid, then brush over the whole surface of the dried sheet. Now place the second sheet directly on top the first and brush the liquid over that surface. Continue this until all five layers are covered. The dried bean curd sheets are very fragile, so brush gently. Allow the liquid to saturate completely the five layers for about a half-hour.

STEP 2:

When the liquid is absorbed, start at one end and very tightly roll up the layered sheets. With a length of string, wind around and around the completed roll and tie.

STEP 3:

Place the roll on a plate in the top section of a steamer over boiling water and cover. Steam for 45 minutes. Remove from the steamer, cool and then store in the refrigerator. When ready to serve, untie the string and cut into very thin circular slices.

Serves four.

Straw Mushrooms with Bean Curd
🔁 Choo Goo Geu Dow Fu 🔁

HAVE READY:

vegetable oil

2 squares bean curd, about 3" squares, 1" thick (cut each square into ½" thicknesses; then cut each square diagonally across corners to make an X, forming 4 triangles for a total of 16 triangles)

1 8-ounce can straw mushrooms, drained and rinsed in cold water (dry on paper towels; set aside)

¼ cup canned sliced bamboo shoots, drained and dried

½ teaspoon salt

¼ teaspoon monosodium glutamate (optional)

1 teaspoon dark soy sauce

1 teaspoon light soy sauce

1 teaspoon cornstarch blended with 2 tablespoons water

STEP 1:

Measure 2 inches of oil in a deep-fry pan. Preheat to 350° F. Test for readiness by tossing in a small piece of bread—if it pops up to the surface immediately, the oil is ready. Add four of the triangles of bean curd at a time. Turn each over and immediately remove. Drain on paper towels. Repeat until all sixteen are lightly deep-fried but not crisp.

STEP 2:

Preheat wok and heat 2 tablespoons oil. Add the straw mushrooms and bamboo shoots, and stir for 1 minute. Then add the fried bean curd and mix thoroughly. Now add the salt, monosodium glutamate and soy sauces, mix, and pour in the cornstarch blend. Mix thoroughly and serve immediately.

Serves four.

Steamed Eggplant
🔁 Jing Keh 🔁

HAVE READY:
1 large eggplant (slice off stem end and cut eggplant into 6 wedges)
2 tablespoons vegetable oil
1 green onion with 6 inches of stem (thin-slice diagonally into 2-inch pieces)
1 tablespoon light Chinese soy sauce
1 tablespoon dark Chinese soy sauce
dash salt
dash pepper
¼ teaspoon sugar
¼ teaspoon M.S.G.

METHOD:
Steam the eggplant, covered, for 30 minutes over boiling water. Remove from fire. Coat bottom and sides of preheated wok or skillet with oil, and when oil is hot, first add the onion and quick-fry a few seconds. Then add the eggplant, soy sauces, salt, sugar, pepper and M.S.G., stir-fry for 2 or 3 minutes. Serve immediately.

Serves four.

Buddha's Dish
🜚 Lo Hon Chai 🜚

(A favorite of vegetarian monks in China)

HAVE READY:

4 squares bean curd (from Chinese market)

2 tablespoons dark Chinese soy sauce

2 teaspoons light Chinese soy sauce

¼ teaspoon Five-Spice Powder

1 teaspoon sugar

½ teaspoon M.S.G. (optional)

2 tablespoons vegetable oil

¼ cup green onion with 6 inches of stem

½ cup black soaked mushrooms

½ cup carrots sliced-thin vertically

½ cup bell peppers, thin-sliced

¼ cup green chili pepper

½ cup canned bamboo shoots

STEP 1:

Put the 4 squares bean curd on a towel placed on a cutting board. Place another towel on top. Put something heavy like two telephone directories on top and leave overnight to squeeze out all the moisture, leaving compact squares about ¼-inch thick.

STEP 2:

Marinate bean squares in mixture of 1 tablespoon of dark soy sauce, 1 teaspoon light soy sauce, Five-Spice Powder, ½ teaspoon sugar and ¼ teaspoon M.S.G. for 2 hours.

STEP 3:

Preheat oven to a high temperature, put the marinated bean curd on a pan into the oven, then immediately lower heat to 200° F., baking for 2 or 3 hours in order to dry out completely the curd. Cool in the refrigerator before slicing. When cool, slice each square into two separate squares, then put one on top of the other and slice as thin as you can in strips. Set aside.

STEP 4:
Coat the bottom and sides of a preheated wok with 2 tablespoons vegetable oil. Quick-fry the green onion and black mushrooms for 1 minute, add the bean curds for 1 minute, then stir in the carrots and peppers and fry for 1 more minute.

STEP 5:
Now add the bamboo shoots, 1 tablespoon dark soy sauce, 1 teaspoon light soy sauce, ½ teaspoon sugar and ¼ teaspoon M.S.G., stir and serve immediately.

Serves four.

Quick Fried Cabbage
↲↳ Chow Wong Nga Bak Choy ↲↳

HAVE READY:

1 head American cabbage	2 tablespoons dark Chinese soy sauce
3 tablespoons vegetable oil	1 teaspoon light Chinese soy sauce
1 green onion plus 4 inches of the stem, chopped	1 teaspoon sugar
	¼ teaspoon M.S.G. (optional)
½ cup water	

STEP 1:
Wash cabbage thoroughly and dry. Slice in half, cut out core and discard. Cut each half into thirds, then each third into chunks.

STEP 2:
Preheat wok and cover bottom and sides with 3 tablespoons oil. Over high heat, stir-fry the chopped onion a few seconds, add cabbage and quick-fry for 1 minute.

STEP 3:

Add the soy sauces, sugar and M.S.G., stirring in. Then add the water, stir and cover. Cook over high heat for 10 minutes. Remove and serve on platter.

Serves four.

Quick Fried Lettuce
🜨 Chow Sang Choy 🜨

HAVE READY:
     1 head lettuce sliced into 6 parts
  3½ tablespoons vegetable oil
     2 large green onions with white part of stem,
         cut into diagonal slivers
     1 teaspoon salt
   ¼ cup water
     1 dash M.S.G. (optional)

METHOD:

Preheat wok or skillet, then add the vegetable oil, coating bottom and sides. Add the lettuce and onions, and stir-fry for about 1 minute. Add salt, water and M.S.G. and stir well. Cover and quick-fry over medium heat for 2 minutes.

Remove with a slotted spoon so that the liquid drains back into the pan.

Serves four.

Spinach with Bamboo Shoots
🧧 Juk Suhn Chow Bo Choy 🧧

HAVE READY:

2 tablespoons vegetable oil	1 teaspoon salt
1 ¼" slice fresh ginger root	½ teaspoon sugar
	¼ teaspoon M.S.G. (optional)
1 package fresh spinach (already cleaned)	1 cup sliced canned bamboo shoots

(If spinach needs to be washed, be sure to dry it on paper toweling before pan-frying.)

STEP 1:
Preheat wok and swirl oil around the bottom and sides. Stir-fry the ginger slice to flavor the oil, then remove the ginger and discard. Add the spinach, stirring as it fries, for 4 minutes.

STEP 2:
Add salt, sugar, M.S.G. and bamboo shoots, quick-frying for 1 minute, stirring well. Now lift the spinach from the wok to drain it, then serve.

Serves four generously.

Broccoli Garnished with Ham
🧧 Foh Toi Chow Gai Lan Choy 🧧

HAVE READY:

1½ pounds fresh broccoli	½ teaspoon sugar (optional)
2 tablespoons oil	1½ teaspoons cornstarch
1 clove garlic	
1 teaspoon salt	1 cup finely chopped cooked ham
1½ cups water	

STEP 1:
Cut the broccoli into 3" pieces from top of floweret to stem. Cut away tough skin and leaves.

Wash and drain. In a preheated wok or skillet over high heat, put 2 tablespoons oil and coat bottom and sides. Rub the garlic over the bottom and sides, then discard the garlic. Add salt, then the broccoli, and stir for 2 minutes.

STEP 2:

Stir in 1 cup water and ½ teaspoon sugar. Cover and cook over high heat for 5 minutes. (Do not lift up cover—the broccoli will lose its bright green color and turn yellow.)

STEP 3:

Make a blend of the cornstarch with ½ cup water. Remove the broccoli to a serving dish, and, to the liquid remaining in the wok, add the cornstarch mixture and allow it to thicken. Add the chopped ham and stir 1 minute, then spoon over the broccoli.

Serves four generously.

Red Cabbage with Hot & Sour Sauce
🔁 Suen Lat Hung Yea Choy 🔁

HAVE READY:

2 tablespoons vege- table oil
¼ cup thin-sliced green onion and stem
1 head of red cabbage (wash, cut into quarters, remove hard core, then cut each cabbage section horizontally into thirds)

¼ cup water
1 tablespoon dark Chinese soy sauce
2 tablespoons wine vinegar
1 teaspoon Tabasco sauce
1 teaspoon sugar
¼ teaspoon mono- sodium glutamate (optional)

STEP 1:

Preheat wok, add oil, and when hot, stir-fry the onion for just a few seconds, then add the cabbage. Stir-fry for 1 minute, then add water and cover for 1 minute.

STEP 2:
In a small bowl, blend the soy sauce, vinegar, Tabasco sauce, sugar and monosodium glutamate. Uncover the cabbage, add the sauces, stir to blend thoroughly (about 1 minute) and remove to a serving dish.

Serves four.

Hot & Sour String Beans with Carrots & Celery
🔁 Sai Khun Hung Loh Bak 🔁

HAVE READY:

3 tablespoons vegetable oil

2 tablespoons thin-sliced green onion and stem

1 cup fresh string beans (remove strings, thin-slice into 2-inch lengths)

½ cup carrots, diagonally sliced into 2-inch lengths

¼ cup hot green pepper, thin-sliced (optional)

1 teaspoon salt

2 tablespoons water

1 cup celery sticks, diagonally sliced into 2-inch strips

1 cup dried bean curd (sold in cellophane packages of four in Chinese markets. Slice each square into half horizontally, then thin-slice.)

½ teaspoon thin Chinese soy sauce

1 tablespoon white vinegar

½ teaspoon sugar

¼ teaspoon monosodium glutamate (optional)

METHOD:
In a preheated wok, heat the oil. When hot, add the onion, then immediately add the string beans, carrots and hot pepper. Stir-fry about 1 minute. Add the salt and water, stir another

minute. Now add the celery and bean curd, stir 1 minute, and finally put in the soy sauce, wine vinegar, sugar and monosodium glutamate, and stir evenly. Remove to platter and serve immediately.

Serves four.

Asparagus with Black Bean Sauce
🔁 Dow See Chow Lu Suhn 🔁

HAVE READY:

- 2 tablespoons vegetable oil
- 2 cloves garlic, crushed
- 1 tablespoon canned black bean sauce
- 2 cups asparagus tips and tender stalks, thin-sliced diagonally into 1½ inch lengths
- 3 tablespoons water
- 1 tablespoon dark Chinese soy sauce
- 1 cup dried Chinese bean curd, sliced in half horizontally, then thin-sliced
- ½ teaspoon sugar
- ¼ teaspoon monosodium glutamate (optional)

METHOD:

Preheat the wok, then add the vegetable oil. When hot, rub the crushed garlic over the bottom and sides, remove and discard the garlic. Add the black bean sauce, then the asparagus; stir-fry for 1 minute. Stir in the water and soy sauce, and cover for 1 minute. Remove cover, add the bean curd and stir-fry for another minute. Now put in the sugar and monosodium glutamate, stir in evenly and remove to a platter.

Serves four.

Pea Pods with Black Mushrooms
🔁 Ho Lan Dow Chow Dung Goo 🔁

HAVE READY:

1 cup dried whole black mushrooms (wash thoroughly, rinse and soak for 2 hours in warm water; remove from water, but reserve this water for the recipe, then dry mushrooms on paper toweling and cut off tough stems)

3 tablespoons vegetable oil

2 slices ¼" ginger root, pared

7 tablespoons of reserve water (from mushrooms)

½ teaspoon salt

1 teaspoon thin Chinese soy sauce

2 cups pea pods with strings removed

1 teaspoon cornstarch

1 teaspoon sugar

¼ teaspoon monosodium glutamate (optional)

STEP 1:

In a preheated wok, add the vegetable oil. When hot, swirl the ginger root around the bottom and sides, remove and discard the ginger. Add the mushrooms and stir-fry for about 2 minutes. Add 1 tablespoon of the reserve water, salt and soy sauce. Stir for 1 minute, then add the pea pods. Stir-fry for 2 minutes, then add 3 more tablespoons of the reserve water.

STEP 2:

In a small bowl, blend 3 tablespoons of the mushroom water, the cornstarch, sugar and monosodium glutamate. Add this to the wok mixture and stir in well. Remove to platter and serve immediately.

Serves four.

Shanghai Chicken Salad
↻ Sheung Hoi Gai Salad ↻

HAVE READY:

- 1 cup fresh bean sprouts, with end threads removed
- 1 cup celery, diagonally-cut and thin-sliced into 2" lengths
- 1 cup pre-soaked, drained Agar Agar cut into 3" lengths before soaking
- 1 teaspoon sesame oil
- 1 tablespoon dark soy sauce
- 1 tablespoon light soy sauce
- 1 teaspoon sugar
- 2 teaspoons wine vinegar
- ¼ teaspoon M.S.G. (optional)
- ¼ teaspoon Tabasco sauce
- 1 cup pre-cooked, cold chicken meat, thin-sliced
- ½ head shredded lettuce

STEP 1:

In boiling water sufficient to cover them, add the bean sprouts and celery slices. Immediately turn off the heat and blanch in the boiling water for 1 minute. Remove, drain in colander with cold tap water, drain well and dry on paper toweling. Chill in refrigerator until cold; if possible, chill overnight.

STEP 2:

In a large salad bowl, add the sesame oil, soy sauces, sugar, wine vinegar, M.S.G. and Tabasco sauce. Mix well, then stir in the chicken. Add the cold bean sprouts, celery and Agar Agar, toss well and serve on a bed of shredded lettuce.

Serves four.

Shredded Chicken & Cucumber Salad

🔁 Gai See Wong Kwa 🔁

(Just as the Chinese Hot Pot is a wonderful dish for cold weather, this shredded chicken and cucumber salad is ideal for a hot summer night. Not only is it cool and refreshing, but it also uses leftovers and requires no cooking over a hot stove.)

HAVE READY:

1 cup left-over chicken	1 teaspoon sugar
2 cucumbers	¼ teaspoon mono-
1 tablespoon dark	sodium glutamate
Chinese soy sauce	(optional)
1 teaspoon thin	1 cup shredded lettuce
Chinese soy sauce	(optional)
1 tablespoon red wine	
vinegar	

STEP 1:

Tear the pieces of left-over chicken into long shreds. Pare the cucumbers, slice them in half lengthwise and remove the seeds and the center section. Shred to the same size as the chicken.

STEP 2:

In a mixing bowl, blend the soy sauces, wine vinegar, sugar and monosodium glutamate. Add the chicken and cucumber shreds, and stir thoroughly.

STEP 3:

Arrange the lettuce to form a bed on a platter or a salad bowl chilled in the refrigerator. Spoon the chicken/cucumber mixture over and serve.

Serves four.

Pea Pods with Water Chestnuts
🔃 Ho Lan Dow Chow Ma Tai 🔃

(This is a dish you should feature during the season for pea pods because the price varies then from 65¢ per pound up to $3.50 per pound when they are out of season.)

HAVE READY:

- 2 tablespoons vegetable oil
- 1 ¼" slice ginger root
- 1 pound Chinese pea pods, washed, dried, with strings removed from both ends
- 1 teaspoon salt
- 1 tablespoon water
- 1 cup canned thin-sliced water chestnuts
- ½ teaspoon sugar

METHOD:

In a preheated wok, heat the vegetable oil over high heat. Swirl the ginger root around the sides and bottom, remove and discard the ginger. Add the pea pods and stir-fry for just a few seconds before adding the salt and water. Cover the wok and reduce heat to medium; cook for a few seconds. Remove the cover, add the water chestnuts and the sugar, stir-fry for 1 minute and serve immediately.

Serves four.

This is one of the favorite dishes in my restaurant, for reasons I can't explain. Perhaps it is because of the fresh green color.

Jellyfish & Cucumber Salad

🔁 Hai Jit Wong Kwa Salad 🔁

HAVE READY:

- 2 cups shredded jellyfish
- 6 tablespoons wine vinegar
- 4 teaspoons sugar
- ½ teaspoon salt
- 1 teaspoon sesame oil
- 1 tablespoon light soy sauce
- 1 tablespoon dark soy sauce
- ¼ teaspoon monosodium glutamate
- 2 cucumbers (pare and cut in half lengthwise, carve out the seed section, and cut into thin slices crosswise)

STEP 1:

Soak one-half of the half-pound package of jellyfish in warm (not hot) water overnight. Drain carefully and rinse off salt. Cut into thin strips about 2 inches long.

STEP 2:

Mix the vinegar, sugar, salt, sesame oil, soy sauces and monosodium glutamate. Add the jellyfish and cucumbers, and mix thoroughly. Chill in the refrigerator for several hours before serving.

Serves four.

Egg Dishes

The Chinese have a high regard for the egg, not only because of its health-giving contents but also because the egg is one of the representations of Yin and Yang, the negative and positive principles of universal life.

The Yin-Yang symbol above was taken from the egg, the white of the egg symbolizing the Yang or positive, the yolk symbolizing the Yin or negative.

The white (Yang) is maleness, the yolk (Yin) is femaleness. One is the sun, the other the moon; one is light and the other darkness. Heaven is one, earth is the other.

The next time you see an egg, take a closer look. According to the Chinese, it's all there.

Steamed Three-Egg Rainbow
杂 Jing Tsai Dahn 杂

(If this dish is waiting for other dishes to be completed, remove the cover but let it stay in the steamer with the flame off.)

HAVE READY:
- 2 Thousand Year Eggs
- 2 Salted Eggs
- 4 uncooked eggs
- 1 can chicken broth, fat skimmed off
- ½ teaspoon vegetable oil
- 1 green onion and stem, chopped fine

STEP 1:
Remove the clay and shells from the Thousand Year Eggs and dice. The Salted Eggs have a firm yolk but raw egg whites, so to remove the outer black coating, crack the eggs and separate the egg whites from the firm yolks. Dice these yolks with the Thousand Year yolks.

STEP 2:
Break the 4 uncooked eggs into a bowl and beat slightly with a fork. Add the egg whites from the Salted Eggs, the broth, vegetable oil and the diced egg mixture. Stir together in a bowl.

STEP 3:
Bring water to boil in the bottom of a steamer. Put the bowl in the top section, reduce to minimum heat, cover and steam for 10 to 15 minutes, or until the eggs are set and custardy. Garnish with onion slices and serve hot.

Serves four.

Golden Coin Eggs
🔄 Gum Chien Dahn 🔄

(Served with a congee, this is a typical Chinese breakfast item.)

HAVE READY:
  1 tablespoon vegetable oil
  8 eggs
    salt
  4 teaspoons oyster sauce

STEP 1:
In a preheated skillet, put 1 tablespoon oil and spread it evenly over the bottom of the pan. Reduce to moderate heat. Break each egg into a saucer separately, then slip each one into the skillet, doing four eggs at a time, or as many as you can handle in your skillet. Sprinkle eggs lightly with salt. Now pour ½ teaspoon oyster sauce over each egg.

STEP 2:
As soon as the edges brown slightly but the whites are still moist, flip over half of the egg white with a spatula to form a half-moon shape. Press the edges lightly to seal. Turn over for 1 second, then carefully convey to a platter. Be sure not to overcook the egg whites.

Serves four.

This recipe brings back memories of my childhood. I had a rather long siege of illness and my grandfather served me a raw egg broken over a hot congee— he believed uncooked eggs were the most beneficial.

Steamed Three Eggs

卍 Jing Sam Dahn 卍

(This makes an excellent appetizer course or a cold dish.)

HAVE READY:
- 1 Thousand Year egg
- 1 salted egg
- 3 uncooked eggs
- ½ teaspoon salt

STEP 1:

Remove the clay from the shell of the Thousand Year egg, then peel away the shell, since the egg is already cooked. Dice it.

STEP 2:

Salted eggs have a firm yolk, but a raw egg white. Remove the outer black coating, crack the egg and separate the egg white from the firm yolk. Dice the yolk.

STEP 3:

Break the 3 fresh eggs into a bowl, add the salt and the uncooked salted egg white. Beat with a fork.

STEP 4:

Bring water to boil in the bottom of a steamer. Mix the diced eggs into the uncooked egg mixture and spoon into an oblong pan which will fit in the top of the steamer. Steam 15 minutes over continuously boiling water, or until the mixture is firm and dry. Remove the pan, let cool and then cut into bite-sized squares just before serving. You may prepare it before-hand, refrigerate, and cut just before serving.

Serves four.

Egg Foo Yung
🔁 Foo Yung Dahn 🔁

HAVE READY:

1 teaspoon light Chinese soy sauce	1 cup bean sprouts, threads removed
¼ teaspoon salt	¼ cup white onion, cut in thin strips
1 dash M.S.G. (optional)	¼ cup canned mush-rooms, sliced thin
1 cup barbecued pork, cut in thin strips	4 eggs
	1 teaspoon vegetable oil

STEP 1:

In a large bowl, mix the soy sauce, salt and M.S.G. Add the pork, bean sprouts, onions, mushroom, and mix well. Break the eggs (don't beat them) into the mixture and lightly stir-toss.

STEP 2:

Pour the teaspoon oil on the stove grill. When it is hot, spoon the mixture onto the grill in circles the size of a hamburger. Brown one side, turn with a spatula; then brown the other side, for about 2 minutes on each side. Remove and serve.

Serves four.

Shrimp Scrambled Eggs
🔁 Har Yan Chow Dahn 🔁

HAVE READY:

4 tablespoons oil	deveined and cut into 4 pieces
1 ½" fresh peeled ginger root slice	8 eggs
1 teaspoon salt pinch pepper	¼ cup finely chopped green onion
1 cup uncooked shrimp,	½ cup frozen peas

STEP 1:

Coat preheated wok or skillet with 1 tablespoon oil. Rub the ginger over the sides and bottom to flavor the oil, then discard the ginger. Add ¼ teaspoon salt and pinch of pepper. Over high heat quick-fry the shrimp for 3 minutes. Remove from the skillet and set aside.

STEP 2:

Break the eggs into a bowl, add ½ teaspoon salt and beat well.

STEP 3:

Wash and preheat the wok or skillet and coat bottom and sides with 3 tablespoons oil. Add the chopped onion and peas, cooking over high heat for a few seconds. Add the eggs and stir while they cook for several seconds, then add the shrimp, stir and serve.

Serves four.

Tea Eggs
🔃 Char Yip Dahn 🔃

HAVE READY:
   1 dozen eggs
      water to cover
   ¼ cup black tea leaves
   2 cloves star anise
   2 teaspoons salt
   1 teaspoon thin
      Chinese soy sauce
   1 tablespoon dark
      Chinese soy sauce

STEP 1:

Place eggs in water to cover and bring to a boil over medium heat; reduce heat and cook for 10 minutes. Reserve the water. Run cold tap water over the eggs until cooled, then roll each egg on a paper towel to dry. Now tap each egg gently with a spoon to crack the shell, but do not remove the shell.

STEP 2:
Bring the reserved water to a boil again. If there is not enough water to cover the eggs, add more. Now put in the tea leaves, star anise, salt and the soy sauces, then the eggs. Cover and simmer for about 1 hour until the eggs turn brown. Turn off the heat and let the eggs stand covered for 30 minutes.

STEP 3:
Drain the eggs, cool and shell. When the eggs are finished, they will look like marbelized porcelain. Before serving, cut into quarters and arrange in flower-petal style on a plate.

It was the custom when I was growing up in China to serve these eggs to any guests who dropped by during the two weeks of the New Year holiday. Now we serve them as a tea delicacy. They are also good to take on picnics, left in their shells until ready to eat.

New Baby Red Eggs
🔁 Hung Gai Dahn 🔁

(Eggs are a symbol of fertility in China, and red is considered a lucky symbol. Whenever there is a birth in the family, the proud father presents his friends one of these hardboiled red eggs instead of a cigar.)

HAVE READY:
- 1 **dozen eggs**
  water to cover
- 30 **drops red food coloring (or red Easter egg dye)**
- 1 **teaspoon vinegar**
- 1 **cup boiling water**

STEP 1:

Place the eggs in a 2-quart pot, cover with water and bring to a boil over medium heat. Reduce to simmer and cook for 10 to 15 minutes. Remove eggs from the pot and dry on paper toweling.

STEP 2:

Bring 1 cup of water to a boil, add 1 teaspoon vinegar and the food coloring, and stir to dissolve. Pour the dye into a bowl deep enough so that each egg will be submerged completely, one at a time. Dye each egg until it is pinkish red.

Rice & Noodle Dishes

Subgum Fried Rice
🔁 Sub Gum Chow Fan 🔁

(This rice dish is usually found in all gourmet dinners served by Cantonese restaurants. Its name derives from the city Subgum, where the dish originated.)

HAVE READY:

- 2 tablespoons vegetable oil
- ¼ cup green onions with stem, chopped
- 2 eggs, slightly beaten
- ¼ cup green peas, uncooked
- ¼ cup cooked shrimp, diced
- 3 cups cold cooked rice
- ¼ cup barbecued pork or cooked ham, diced
- ½ teaspoon salt
- 1 teaspoon light soy sauce
- 1 tablespoon dark soy sauce

METHOD:

Preheat the wok and heat the oil. Add onions and eggs, quick-fry, then add peas and shrimp and blend together. Immediately add the rice, press gently to the sides and bottom to separate the kernels, then the pork, salt and soy sauces. Mix together quickly and serve.

Serves four.

Egg Fried Rice
🔁 Gai Dahn Chow Fan 🔁

HAVE READY:

- 3 tablespoons vegetable oil
- 1 cup chopped green onion and stem
- 2 beaten eggs
- 3 cups cold cooked rice
- 1 tablespoon dark soy sauce
- ½ teaspoon salt
- ¼ teaspoon mono- sodium glutamate (optional)

180

METHOD:

Preheat the wok. Heat the oil. When hot, add the onion and eggs and stir quickly. Immediately add the rice, gently pressing it to the sides and bottom to separate the kernels. Add the soy sauce, salt and monosodium glutamate. Stir and serve immediately.

Serves four.

This dish is very popular in all Chinese restaurants. Whenever actor Pat O'Brien is in my restaurant, he insists on ordering "burnt rice." At first the captain and waiter tending the actor's table had a difficult time with the chef, who firmly refused to burn the rice. I finally went into the kitchen myself to solve the impasse, directing the chef to simply add two more tablespoons of dark soy sauce which will not spoil the taste and gives the rice a burned color.

Turkey & Beef Congee
🔃 Foh Gai Ngau Yoke Chuk 🔃

(This recipe is served for breakfast or for a light supper or late snack after the theatre. It can be prepared hours ahead and be reheated.)

HAVE READY:

1 left-over turkey carcass, after most of the meat has been sliced off	1 pound ground round steak
	1 tablespoon dark soy sauce
water to cover in a 5-quart pot with lid	2 teaspoons light soy sauce
1 cup uncooked white rice, washed thoroughly	1 teaspoon salt
	1 teaspoon cornstarch

STEP 1:

Put the turkey in a large lidded pot and cover with water. Bring to a boil and when it reaches the boiling stage, skim off the fat. Place two wooden chopsticks over the oven top, then place the lid on top. Simmer for 2 hours. Now add the rice and continue to simmer for 2 more hours, skimming off fat from time to time. After 4 hours, discard the bones from the congee stock with a slotted spoon. Cover and set aside.

STEP 2:

Marinate for a few minutes the ground beef with the soy sauces, salt and cornstarch.

STEP 3:

Just before serving, reheat. If the congee is too thick, bring it to a boil and add an additional cup of water, bringing it again to a boil. Add the marinated beef, stir in thoroughly and serve immediately.

Serves four.

Crisp Noodles
↻ Leun Mein Wong Chow Mein ↻

HAVE READY:
  2 quarts vegetable oil
  1 pound Chinese egg noodles (or substitute Italian-style egg noodles)

STEP 1:

Pour the vegetable oil into a deep-fryer and heat to 400° F. To test for readiness, drop a strand of a noodle into the oil. If it sinks to the bottom, the oil is not hot enough. When it pops to the surface immediately, the oil is ready.

STEP 2:

Deep-fry a third of the noodles at a time until they are golden brown. After draining on paper towels, break into approximately 1½ inch lengths.

These can also be served as an appetizer with cocktails.

If you want rice softer, add more water.

If you want it cooked harder, use less water and a shorter time to simmer.

If you set the heat very low, you can leave the rice and go ahead with other cooking.

To make Fun See (thread noodles) come out very soft—not too soft or they will stick together—you soak them in less time and cook them quickly.

To make Fun See soft, soak and cook longer.

The same is true for cooking egg noodles.

White Rice & Ham Fried Rice
↻ Foh Toi Chow Fan ↻

WHITE RICE

HAVE READY:
   2 cups long grain white rice
   2 cups hot or boiling water

METHOD:
Wash rice, drain and put in a 2-quart pot. Add the water and cover, cooking over high heat. When rice reaches the boiling stage, remove cover and stir just enough to keep the rice from sticking to the sides and bottom. Continue cooking, uncovered, over high heat until the water has almost all boiled away. Now cover the pot and turn the burner down to very low heat, letting the rice simmer for about 15 minutes. Don't peek!

Serves four.

FRIED RICE

HAVE READY:

rice (prepare the night before as in above recipe)

2 tablespoons vegetable oil

2 heaping tablespoons chopped green onion

2 eggs, beaten well

½ cup diced cooked ham

1 tablespoon light soy sauce

1 tablespoon dark soy sauce (optional for coloring)

METHOD:

Preheat skillet and coat bottom and sides with oil. Over high heat quick-fry the onions for 2 seconds, then stir in eggs for 2 seconds. Add ham, rice and soy sauces, mixing well, and continue to stir for about 3 minutes.

Serves four.

Turkey Congee
🔃 Foh Gai Chuk 🔃

(This recipe is served for breakfast or for a light supper or late snack after the theatre. It can be prepared hours ahead and be reheated.)

HAVE READY:

1 leftover turkey carcass (cut off most of the meat in thin slices and set aside in a bowl; use enough water to cover the carcass in a 5-quart pot with lid)

1 cup uncooked white

rice, washed thoroughly

1 tablespoon dark soy sauce

2 teaspoons thin soy sauce

1 teaspoon salt

2 tablespoons chopped green onions

1 teaspoon sesame oil

STEP 1:

Put the turkey into a large lidded pot and cover with water. Bring to a boil and when it reaches the boiling stage, skim off the fat. Place two wooden chopsticks over the open top, then place the lid on the chopsticks. Simmer for 2 hours, then add the rice and continue to simmer for 2 more hours, skimming off the fat from time to time. After 4 hours, discard the bones from the congee stock with a slotted spoon. Cover and set aside.

STEP 2:

Just before serving, reheat to a boil and add an additional cup of water if the congee is too thick, again bringing it to a boil. Take off the heat and stir in the turkey meat, the soy sauces, salt, onions and sesame oil.

Serves four.

Pan-Fried Noodles with Oyster Sauce
🀄 Hao Yao Chow Mein 🀄

HAVE READY:

- 2 quarts water
- 1 pound Chinese egg noodles (or substitute Italian-style egg noodles)
- 4 tablespoons vegetable oil
- 3 tablespoons oyster sauce
- 1 teaspoon sugar
- ¼ teaspoon monosodium glutamate (optional)
- 2 ¼" slices ginger root, pared

STEP 1:

In a large pot, bring the water to a boil, then drop in noodles and continue boiling for 10 or 15 minutes until tender. Take from the fire, pour noodles into a colander and rinse for several minutes under cold water. Drain and return to the pot, with 1 tablespoon of vegetable oil mixed in to prevent the noodles from sticking.

STEP 2:
Lightly grease the pancake griddle with 1 table-spoon oil. When hot, form the noodles into 6 hamburger-sized patties on the griddle and pan-fry on each side until brown, turning with a skillet. Set aside.

STEP 3:
Blend the oyster sauce, 1 tablespoon water, sugar, and monosodium glutamate in a small bowl. Preheat the wok and add 2 tablespoons oil. When hot, swirl the 2 pieces of ginger root over the bottom and sides, then discard the ginger.

STEP 4:
Add the 6 loosely formed patties and stir with chopsticks or a long fork in such a way that they return to their unbroken lengths, then pour the oyster sauce mixture over them, stirring to coat evenly. Remove to a platter and serve.

Serves four.

Leftover Ham Noodles
🔃 Foh Toi Mein 🔃

HAVE READY:
   2 quarts water
   1 pound Chinese egg noodles (or substitute
        thin noodles or spaghetti)
   2 cans chicken broth with fat skimmed off,
        diluted with 1 can water
   1 cup thin-sliced left-over ham, 2" long, ¼" thick
   1 teaspoon thin Chinese soy sauce
   1 tablespoon diagonally-sliced green onion with stem

STEP 1:
Bring the 2 quarts of water to a boil, add the noodles and cook until soft (about 10 minutes). Drain the noodles in a colander and rinse with cold water under the tap.

STEP 2:
Bring the broth/water dilution to a boil in a 2-quart pot. When boiling, add the drained noodles, return to a boil, then turn off the heat. Add the ham, soy sauce and onion, and serve hot.

Serves four.

Beef Meatball Congee
🐉 Ngau Yoke Chuk 🐉

(This is a good dish to serve after too many rich holiday dinners, as well as for those days when you may not feel too well and want to eat lightly but nourishingly.)

HAVE READY:

1 pound ground lean beef	1 teaspoon vegetable oil
2 tablespoons dark Chinese soy sauce	½ teaspoon sugar
	4 quarts water
2 teaspoons thin Chinese soy sauce	1 cup uncooked rice, washed and drained
1 tablespoon cornstarch	¼ cup chopped green onion and stem (optional)
1 teaspoon salt	
1 teaspoon red cooking wine	1 teaspoon sesame oil

STEP 1:
Marinate the beef for a few minutes in a bowl containing a blend of the soy sauces, cornstarch, salt, wine, vegetable oil and sugar. Mix well and set aside.

187

STEP 2:

Bring the water to a boil over high heat in a large pot. When it reaches the rolling boil stage, add the rice and cook uncovered until it reaches the boiling stage again. Turn the heat to low, place two wooden chopsticks across the top of the pot and place the lid over them. Simmer for 3 hours, then bring to the boiling stage.

STEP 3:

Form the marinated beef into tiny balls the size of marbles and drop them a few at a time into the boiling liquid, stirring slowly. Continue to do this until all the meat balls are in the pot. When they float to the top, they are done (about 5 minutes). Turn off the heat.

Add the green onions and sesame oil, stir and ladle into soup bowls.

Serves four, generously.

Leftover Chicken with Noodles, Shanghai Style
🜨 Gai See Mein 🜨

HAVE READY:

2 quarts water	¼ cup thin-sliced hot green pepper
1 pound Chinese egg noodles (or substitute thin noodles or spaghetti)	1 cup shredded leftover chicken
4 tablespoons vegetable oil	1 tablespoon cornstarch blended with 1 tablespoon water
2 tablespoons dark Chinese soy sauce	1 teaspoon light Chinese soy sauce
½ cup diagonally sliced green onions with stem	¼ teaspoon monosodium glutamate (optional)

STEP 1:

Bring the 2 quarts of water to a boil, add the noodles and cook until soft (about 10 minutes).

Drain the noodles into a colander, rinse under cold water and drain.

STEP 2:
In a preheated wok heat 2 tablespoons vegetable oil over high heat. Add the noodles, stir-fry for 1 minute, then mix in 1 tablespoon dark soy sauce and stir-fry for another minute. Remove to a serving platter.

STEP 3:
Wash, dry and preheat the wok. Heat 2 table-spoons vegetable oil and, when hot, add the onions and hot pepper, and quick-fry for 1 minute. Add the shredded chicken and stir in evenly.

STEP 4:
Mix the cornstarch and water blend with the remaining soy sauces and the monosodium glutamate. Add to the chicken mixture, stir evenly and spoon immediately on top the cooked noodles.

Serves four.

Pork Noodles in Chicken Broth
🔁 Gai Tong Chu Yoke Mein 🔁

HAVE READY:

2 quarts water	1 cup thin-sliced barbecued pork (see barbecued pork recipe) or substitute 1 cup thin-sliced boiled ham)
¼ pound egg noodles	
1 teaspoon vegetable oil	
2 cans chicken broth with fat skimmed off	
½ teaspoon sesame oil	4 teaspoons chopped green onion with stem
1 teaspoon thin Chinese soy sauce	

STEP 1:

Bring 2 quarts of water to a boil in a deep pot. Add the noodles and cook until soft, for about 10 minutes. Remove from the fire, drain the water and soak the noodles in cold water for 10 minutes, then put into a colander and allow to drain thoroughly. Place in a bowl and stir in the teaspoon of vegetable oil to prevent the noodles from sticking together. Set aside.

STEP 2:

Pour the chicken broth and 1 can of water into a pot, then bring to a boil. Add the drained noodles, cook for 1 minute, add the sesame oil and soy sauce and turn off the heat immediately.

STEP 3:

To serve, divide the soup and noodles into four individual bowls and add the pork or ham slices on top. Sprinkle 1 teaspoon of the chopped onion in each bowl as a garnish.

Serves four.

Fried Crab Meat with Noodles

Hai Yoke Chow Mein

HAVE READY:

2 quarts vegetable oil	1 teaspoon salt
1/3 package rice noodles	1/4 teaspoon mono-sodium glutamate
2 slices ginger root, 1/4" thick	1/4 cup chopped cooked Virginia ham
1 small can crab meat	1/4 cup chopped green onion stems for garnish
1 teaspoon white wine	
4 egg whites, unbeaten	
1/4 cup milk	1 bunch Chinese or American parsley
1 teaspoon cornstarch blended with 1 teaspoon water	

STEP 1:

Heat the vegetable oil in a deep-fryer until it reaches 350° F. Test for readiness by dropping one of the noodles into the oil. If it pops up immediately, the oil is ready. Break the noodle skein into three lengths and deep-fry separately. The noodles will explode on contact with the oil, and must be instantly removed before they absorb some of the oil and become soggy. Drain on paper toweling, place on a serving platter and set aside in a warm place.

STEP 2:

In a preheated wok, spoon in 2 tablespoons of the oil from the deep-fryer. When hot, swirl the ginger slices over the bottom and sides, remove and discard the ginger. Add the crab meat and wine, stir-fry for 2 minutes and remove to a bowl.

STEP 3:

Wash and dry the wok. Preheat, and when hot, add 2 more tablespoons from the leftover oil. While it is heating, mix together the unbeaten egg whites, milk, the cornstarch and water blend, salt and monosodium glutamate. Add this mixture to the wok and stir-fry for 1 minute; then add the ham, green onion and crab meat mixture, stir-frying for 10 seconds. Remove and spoon into the center of the platter of fried noodles. Arrange sprigs of parsley as a garnish. Serve immediately.

Serves four.

Desserts

Eight Precious Rice Pudding
🔃 Bahd Bo Fan 🔃

(The name of this dessert refers to eight different kinds of dried fruits and nuts arranged in a decorative design on the bottom of a waxed bowl which, when inverted, becomes the domed top of the pudding. At serving time, a simple hot sauce is poured over it. Although I have listed some Chinese candied fruits and nuts, you may substitute any American varieties for them, such as blanched almond halves, walnuts, or any variety of candied fruits.)

HAVE READY FOR PUDDING:

1 cup glutinous rice
1 cup water
2 tablespoons sugar
2 tablespoons vegetable oil
¾ cup canned sweetened red bean paste
6 pieces each of red and green candied cherries
20 canned lotus seeds (substitute blanched almond halves)
1 tablespoon candied kumquats
6 pieces candied melon
1 tablespoon candied orange peel
2 tablespoons seedless raisins
2 tablespoons seeded dragon eye nuts
10 pitted dates cut in half lengthwise

HAVE READY FOR SYRUP:

1 cup water
1½ tablespoons sugar
2 teaspoons cornstarch blended with 2 tablespoons water

PREPARE PUDDING: STEP 1:

Wash the glutinous rice and rinse several times to remove excess starch. Put into an unbreakable bowl and mix with 1 cup water. Bring the water in the bottom of the steamer to a boil, then place the bowl of rice in the top section, cover and steam for 30 minutes. Remove from the fire and while still hot, add the sugar and mix well.

It is important to work with the rice when it is still hot, so continue with the next step while the rice steams.

STEP 2:
Coat generously with vegetable oil the bottom and sides of a 7" diameter oven-proof bowl. On the bottom arrange the candied fruit in a decorative design—perhaps a flower with petals, leaves and stem—and working outward in circular fashion, arrange the date halves, dragon eye nuts, lotus seeds and raisins in a border.

STEP 3:
Spoon the glutinous rice into the bowl. Pack it tightly against the bottom and sides, but be careful not to disturb your design.

STEP 4:
Mix the vegetable oil with the red bean paste and spread over the rice. Be sure that the bean paste is completely covered with rice or it will run into the rest of the pudding and spoil the appearance.

STEP 5:
Again bring water to a boil in the bottom of the steamer. When it reaches the boiling stage, place the bowl in the top section, cover with the lid and steam for ½ hour.

STEP 6:
Unmold on a decorative plate and serve a side pitcher of syrup with your finished dish. Make the syrup this way:

PREPARE SYRUP:
In a saucepan bring the sugar and a cup of water to a boil, then stir in the cornstarch/water blend and boil a few seconds until the mixture becomes clear and thickens slightly.

Serves four.

King's Almond Delight
🔁 Huang Yan Dow Fu 🔁

HAVE READY:

¼ ounce Agar Agar
(usually packaged
in 4 long pieces;
use one of the
pieces)
3 cups water
3 tablespoons sugar

½ teaspoon almond
extract
2 cups milk
4 teaspoons green
creme de menthe
4 cocktail cherries

STEP 1:

Put the Agar Agar and water in a kettle and heat
over a moderate flame until the Agar Agar is
completely dissolved (15 minutes or less). Add
the sugar. When it is dissolved, turn off the
heat and add the almond extract. Stir evenly. If
the Agar Agar has any sediment in it, strain it
through cheesecloth.

STEP 2:

Add the milk and cool. You can either pour it
into a decorative serving bowl or spoon it into
several individual crystal sherbet glasses.
Refrigerate for several hours.

STEP 3:

Just before serving, pour over the creme de
menthe and center with a red or green cherry.
For a variation, drain a can of fruit cocktail and
pour the fruit over the top. Or garnish with
canned fruit such as pineapple chunks, mandarin
orange sections, cherries, whole loquats or lychee
berries, or a combination of several of these.

STEP 4:

Another way to serve this dish is to chill it in
an oblong pan, then cut into diamond wedges,
squares, or triangles, and spoon it into individual
goblets alternately with chunks of canned fruit.

196

The variations in serving this low-calorie delicious and refreshing dessert are almost endless.

Serves four. (Like any gelatin dessert, it will keep well for days in the refrigerator should you make more than four servings.)

Steamed Lotus with Sweet & Sour Rice
🔃 Lin Gee Noh Maih Fan 🔃

HAVE READY:

2 joined lotus roots, about 5" long (approximately 1 pound)
½ cup glutinous rice
½ cup water
¼ cup sugar
1 tablespoon vegetable oil

½ cup canned cooked chestnuts chopped medium fine (substitute chopped pecan)
1 teaspoon toasted sesame seeds

STEP 1:

Wash the roots and cut them apart. With a sharp knife, peel off the thin skin, then trim off and discard the joined ends. Cut ½" slices off the wider ends to use as caps for the two roots.

STEP 2:

Wash the glutinous rice and rinse several times to remove excess starch. Put into an unbreakable bowl and mix with ½ cup water. Bring the water in the bottom of the steamer to a boil, then place the rice bowl in the top section, cover and steam for 30 minutes. Remove from the fire, and while still hot, add the sugar, oil and chopped chestnuts to the rice, mixing well.

STEP 3:

Allow the mixture to cool slightly. Fill the various-sized holes in the lotus root with the warm rice mixture. If necessary, use a chopstick to push down the rice. When the root is filled, replace the cap and secure with several toothpicks straight down.

STEP 4:

Bring the water in the steamer bottom to a boil again. Place the two roots on an unbreakable dish, set in the top section of the steamer, cover and steam for an hour. Then serve immediately.

(This dish can be used as a dessert after a formal dinner or as a tea delicacy. It is thin-sliced horizontally, placed in overlapping circles on a decorative plate and sprinkled with toasted sesame seeds.)

Serves four to six persons.

Sweet Potato Ball with Red Bean Paste
🔃 Fan Shue Kow Yeun Wu Dow 🔃

(This dish can be served as a dessert or with afternoon tea. The dough can be mixed and kept in a covered jar in the refrigerator for two or three weeks, taking out just what is needed.)

HAVE READY:

3 cups sweet potatoes (cleaned, pared and cut into small pieces) water	2 tablespoons sugar
	1 quart vegetable oil
	1 can sweet red bean paste
1 cup glutinous rice flour (same as glutinous rice powder)	2 tablespoons sesame seeds

STEP 1:

Put the sweet potato pieces in a pot, cover with water and boil until tender. Drain water thoroughly and mash the potatoes. While still hot, sift in the sweet rice flour. It must be mixed hot or the flour will not blend well. Add the sugar and 1 teaspoon vegetable oil, and mix well again. Cool.

STEP 2:

When cool, take a section and roll it between your palms (lightly dusted with flour) and pat it into a flat circle. Put 1 teaspoon of the red bean paste in the center, fold the edges of the patty to the center, then pick it up in your lightly-floured hands and form into the size of a golf ball, or smaller. Cover the bottom of a flat dish with the sesame seeds and roll the balls over the seeds to coat them. Put the balls on a flat sheet covered with aluminium foil to prevent them from sticking to the bottom.

STEP 3:

In a deep-fryer, heat the quart of oil to 350° F. Reduce the heat to low, drop three or four balls at a time into the hot oil and fry until golden brown and they come up to the surface; turn so they will brown evenly (about 10 minutes). Drain on paper towels and serve hot.

Serves four.

Chinese Red Bean Popsicle

🔁 Hung Dow Bing 🔁

HAVE READY:
   1 pound tiny, smooth red beans
      (available in Oriental markets)
      water to cover
   ½ cup brown sugar (or more if you
      prefer a sweeter taste)
      popsicle sticks

STEP 1:

Wash and drain the beans, then put into a soup kettle and cover with water. Cover, bring

199

to a boil, add the sugar, then turn the heat to low and boil 2½ to 3 hours.

STEP 2:
Remove from the heat, allow to cool slightly, then pour the bean mixture through a fine sieve into a large bowl. Allow to cool, then transfer to an ice cube tray and place in the freezer.

STEP 3:
When the mixture starts to congeal, slip popsicle sticks into each square or cube in the tray.

When our children were young, this was their popsicle favorite. It was nutritious because the red beans are healthful, and by making the popsicles myself, I could control the amount of sugar the children ate. They in turn were pleased that I cared enough to make this special treat for them at home.

Apple Glace
🔁 But See Peng Kwo 🔁

HAVE READY:

1 egg white	cubes and cold
¼ cup flour	water for dipping
1 tablespoon cornstarch	1 teaspoon vinegar
⅔ cup water	1 teaspoon sesame
3 apples	seeds
1 quart vegetable oil	serving platter rubbed
¾ cup sugar	with vegetable oil
serving bowl of ice	

STEP 1:
Make a smooth batter with the slightly beaten egg white, flour, cornstarch and ⅓ cup of water. Pare the apples, core and cut each into 6 slices. Dip each slice into the batter to cover.

STEP 2:
Meanwhile, heat the vegetable oil in a deep-fryer to 300° F. Deep-fry the coated apples until pale golden. Drain on paper towels.

STEP 3:

Immediately prepare the syrup. Bring the sugar and ⅓ cup of water to a boil, stirring constantly. When boiling, turn to low heat and stir in 1 tablespoon of vegetable oil. Cook until a small amount dropped from the tip of a spoon into cold water spins a heavy thread and is golden brown. Add the vinegar and stir in.

STEP 4:

By this time you should have the serving platter coated with vegetable oil to keep the apple slices from sticking, and you have the bowl of ice cubes and water brought to the table where the dessert is to be eaten.

SEP 5:

When the syrup is at the thread stage, add the deep-fried apples and mix to coat with the syrup. Remove the apples to the oiled platter and sprinkle sesame seeds over them. Bring to the table and serve immediately.

To eat, pick up the apple slice with chopsticks, fondue fork or regular fork, and dip it for an instant into the ice water to crystalize the sugar into a glace.

Serves four.

Banana Crystal Glace

🔁 But See Heung Jeu 🔁

HAVE READY:

- 4 medium-sized bananas
- 4 tablespoons vegetable oil
- 1 serving bowl of ice cubes and cold water for dipping

- ¾ cup sugar
- ⅓ cup water
- 1 teaspoon vinegar
- 1 tablespoon sesame seeds

STEP 1:

Peel the bananas and cut them into 3 or 4 diagonal slices. Heat the vegetable oil in a skillet at 300° F. Add the bananas and pan-fry until lightly browned on all sides.

STEP 2:

Meanwhile, coat a serving platter with oil so that the banana slices will not stick, and have the bowl of about 12 ice cubes and water ready.

STEP 3:

Combine the sugar and ⅓ cup of water in a pot, bring to a boil slowly, stirring constantly until the mixture spins a heavy thread in cold water. Add the vinegar and stir to mix.

STEP 4:

Dip the bananas into the hot syrup, coat and place on the oiled platter. Sprinkle with the sesame seeds and bring to the serving table immediately.

To eat, pick up a banana slice with chopsticks, fondue fork or regular fork, dip into the ice water to crystallize the syrup, then sample.

Serves four.

Chinese Fruit Bowl

𝕫 Jup Kwo Poon 𝕫

HAVE READY:

2 quarts finely crushed ice (almost like snow)	4 loquats
	4 mandarin orange slices
4 kumquats	4 pineapple chunks
4 lychees	4 candied cherries
16 colored toothpicks	

METHOD:

Place crushed ice in a shallow fruit bowl, pack and invert on a colorful platter or silver tray. Carefully make an indentation with your finger in the ice, put a toothpick in each piece of fruit, and set it in the indentation (otherwise it will slip off). Serve immediately, alone or with cake or ice cream.

(For a variation for a larger gathering, place the fruit in a partially hollowed-out watermelon half, with toothpicks in a small cup on each side. Add watermelon balls.)

Since this is a cookbook, naturally I have not included any recipes for cocktails, but I trust you will forgive me if I suggest one which I think can be an exotic conclusion for a Chinese dinner.

Actually, I have to thank actress Marlo Thomas for introducing me to it, because although it is served at my restaurant, I had never tasted it. Like most Chinese women, I am not much of a cocktail drinker.

Miss Thomas was having dinner with a friend, and as I was chatting with them, the waiter brought a pair of long-stemmed cordial glasses, filled with a golden-brown liquid, with a tiny blue flame on top.

Marlo told me it was called the Harbor Light, and was made of 80% Galliano and 20% Metaxa brandy floating on top. She had gotten the recipe from my bartender and often served the drink at home.

Since then I have suggested the Harbor Light for small private parties in my V.I.P. room, served when the lights are dimmed, and it has been a great success.

Ginger Ice Cream
🔄 Gee Keun Sueh Gou 🔄

HAVE READY:
- ½ gallon vanilla ice cream
- 1 cup chopped candied ginger
- 1 tablespoon liquid ginger (fresh ginger root put into a garlic press)

METHOD:

Remove ice cream from the carton, put into a large bowl and allow it to become soft. When it reaches this stage, add the chopped candied ginger and ginger juice, and mix well.

Return to the ice cream carton and store in the freezer. Allow a week for the ginger flavor to permeate the ice cream thoroughly.

When I asked retired U.S. Air Force General "Jimmy" Doolittle to name his favorite dish, he wrote this note to me: "Jo (his wife) says my favorite dish is Wu's Beef, but hers is your ginger ice cream, so I bow to her."

In my estimation, the Doolittles are living proof of the Chinese adage that "If you love and respect your wife, you will become a successful man."

King's Deep-Fried Milk
🔄 Ng See Chow Ngau Nai 🔄

HAVE READY:

½ cup cornstarch	2 quarts vegetable oil
2½ cups water	2 cups flour
¼ cup evaporated milk	1 teaspoon baking powder
1 teaspoon coconut extract	2 tablespoons powdered sugar
1¼ cups chicken broth (skim off fat)	1 tablespoon toasted sesame seeds (optional)
1 tablespoon butter or margarine	

STEP 1:
  Dilute the cornstarch with ½ cup water. Add the milk and coconut extract, mix well and set aside.

STEP 2:
  Bring the broth and ¾ cup water to a boil. When this reaches the rolling boil stage, reduce the flame and add the cornstarch mixture with the butter. Return to a boil, stirring constantly. Boil for 3 or 4 minutes. Take off flame and pour into a flat container of 8" by 8" (or to a depth of ½" to ¾"). Cool, then refrigerate until it is firm. Cut in bite-sized squares, cubes or rectangles as you prefer.

STEP 3:
  Heat the vegetable oil in a deep-frying pot until it reaches 375° F. Meanwhile, mix the flour, baking powder, ⅔ cup of water and 1 tablespoon oil until it is smooth. When the oil is hot, dip the bite-sized squares into the batter, coating on all sides. Gently dip into the oil and deep-fry until golden brown. Remove and drain on paper toweling. Serve immediately while hot, coating each piece with powdered sugar and perhaps sesame seeds.

  Serves four.

  (The filling can be made and stored covered in the refrigerator for weeks; thus you can serve this dessert on several occasions merely by making a fresh batter and deep-frying.)

My grandfather was born in the city of Ch'ao Ch'ao, which is famous for its tea. Everyone in Ch'ao Ch'ao sipped his tea from small cups, and having one's good tea was an important ritual, often repeated during the day, even though tea then was quite expensive.

On this subject, I remember a story my grandfather told me about a rich man who loved to drink tea. Misfortune fell upon him and he lost all his money. All that remained of his treasures was a small teapot.

However, it was a magical pot because it never required tea. All one had to do was to pour hot water into the pot and the water itself turned into a fragrant tea.

He could have sold the teapot to pay off all his debtors and save his property, but he enjoyed the tea so much that he chose to become a beggar on the street, always keeping his full teapot at his side.

You may doubt the wisdom of his decision, but this little story tells how important tea is in China.

YOUR CHINESE TEA

1. Select the finest grade of tea leaves you can find in a Chinatown market or in a gourmet shop. Be sure it comes in sealed tins, not in plastic or paper containers.
2. Let the water run from the tap until it is fresh, then bring to a boil. If you have bottled or spring water, so much the better.
3. Preheat a four-cup China teapot (never metal

or heavy plastic) and put in one teaspoon of green tea and one teaspoon of black tea. No more!

4. The moment the water comes to a boil, pour it over the tea leaves and cover the teapot.
5. Brew for three to five minutes, then serve.
6. After the tea has been on the table for ten or fifteen minutes, discard tea and make a new pot.

Chinese Hot Pot Cooking

Chinese Hot Pot cooking is the forerunner of the European method of cooking fondue; it means that everyone cooks his own bite-sized servings of food in a bubbling pot of hot broth which is placed in the center of the table.

This is really a fun occasion for you and from four to six of your close friends, especially on a cold night. Invite them to come to your house in very casual clothes so they can sit comfortably on cushions around a low coffee table set in front of a cozy fire. While they sip a small glass of Chinese wine, they pick up a bite-sized piece of raw meat, seafood or fowl with their wooden chopsticks (not plastic or ivory: they lose their shape in the hot broth), dip it into the soup stock, cook it to their preference of doneness, then dip the cooked morsel into the sauce they have fixed for themselves and savor the hot food as well as the relaxed, spontaneous conversation. Two or three hours go by in this delightful manner.

It is an especially good way to spend time with your family. When we lived in New York and our three children were five, six, and eleven, I used to serve a Hot Pot dinner at least once during the two-week period of the Chinese New Year. The children loved it because they could choose just what kind of food they wanted and also because they didn't have to sit as still as they would at the formal dinner table. So, at that time we found that we could put one or two bits of old Chinese philosophy into their heads without giving them a sermon.

No entertaining could be more enjoyable for the host than a Hot Pot meal; the great advantage is

that all the preparations are done in advance.
In fact, you as the host might have the whole day
of the party in which to relax because all the
thin-slicing of the food can be done the day
before, attractively arranged on serving plates
and stored in the refrigerator until party time.
Minutes before the guests arrive, you open several
cans of chicken broth, mix with water, then
bring to a boil on your stove and the soup stock
is ready. Then all you need do is to set out the
plates of uncooked food, the Master Sauce and
the tray of extra condiments, arrange them
around the central electric pot, plug it in, and as
the saying goes, the soup is on!

You will notice that I have made no mention of
the traditional firepot, and for good reason. Since
this book is based on sensible, easy-to-do
Chinese cooking, I would suggest that instead of
the ancient charcoal-burning firepot, you make
things easy for yourself and substitute the electric
casserole or the fondue pot.

When I describe the authentic firepot and tell
you the history behind it as well as explaining
how to use it, you will understand why I recommend the more modern method.

The firepot is a copper pot with a chimney or
funnel rising through the center from a built-in
base below where the charcoals are burned.
Surrounding the funnel is a container for the
broth. The neighboring Mongols brought the
firepot with them when they invaded northern
China, and this pot was adopted by the Chinese
for cooking the lamb and mutton native to their
region. The fame of firepot cooking spread
throughout China, where less pungent meats,
seafood and fowl were substituted for the
aromatic lamb. In those areas it was renamed
the Chinese Hot Pot.

This tradition of being fed bits of wisdom at the meal table dates back to my childhood, when my grandfather would tell us stories with a moral while we ate. One I particularly remember concerned an old emperor who had a young concubine he unwisely loved, for she was vain and willful, and seldom deigned to smile and be happy. He tried in many ways to amuse her in order to make her laugh, but to no avail.

A huge iron bell stood in the center of the palace courtyard, to be rung only if danger was imminent. When the bell was tolled, it would bring in hundreds of soldiers running from all directions to save the emperor. The old ruler decided it might amuse his little doll-girl to see the action which would follow if the bell were rung. He commanded his servant to ring it, and she not only smiled but also laughed outright to see the armed soldiers scampering in to protect their emperor. Then he told the troops to leave—it was nothing.

Several days later he ordered the bell to be rung again, and again the palace swarmed with soldiers, and again it was a false alarm. Yet the emperor had made his concubine laugh once again.

But one day an alert guard, seeing the enemy approaching the city, ran into the courtyard and rang the bell, but this time no one came, and so the emperor and the concubine were killed and the city overtaken.

Such stories reflecting basic truths have been told in different languages to small children all over the world. I'm sure that you recognize my grandfather's fable as the Oriental version of "Cry Wolf."

If you still intend to use the traditional firepot, which you can buy either in a Chinese hardware store or perhaps in your supermarket, it will be necessary first to heat the charcoal briquets in your oven. Put them in the broiler and heat for 12 to 15 minutes until they are red hot, then transfer them with tongs to the funnel of the firepot. It will be necessary to keep a reserve supply heating in the broiler so that the temperature of the firepot will not drop as the original coals diminish their intensity.

At the same time bring the chicken broth to a boil on top of the stove and transfer enough of the hot broth to reach the midway mark in the firepot. It will be necessary to replenish the broth from time to time, whether you use the old-fashioned method or modern electric cookery.

A wide variety of raw meat, fish, fowl and vegetables, cut paper-thin, are placed on pots around the cooking pot (which has an asbestos pad under it), within easy reach of each diner. Also within easy reach is a bowl of Master Sauce and a tray of additional condiments with which each can create his own brand of dipping sauce in a small bowl placed in front of him.

The diner, with chopsticks, fondue fork or wire mesh scoop, picks up one piece of food at a time, immerses it in the stock until it changes color (just several seconds for everything but pork which takes a minute or two). Usually the diner holds onto it while it is cooking, then dips it into his bowl into which he has first broken an egg (a cooling and coating agent) before adding the Master Sauce and the condiments.

The general procedure is to cook all the main ingredients first. Then the vegetables such as celery, cabbage, cellophane noodles, bean curd and spinach are placed in the pot at once, with each diner serving himself. Lastly we come to my favorite part of the meal: each person spoons the greatly enriched soup stock into his bowl to mix with the remainder of his sauce, and drinks it up!

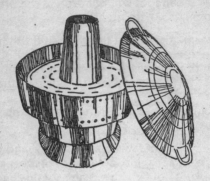

Chinese Hot Pot
🔃 Foh Woh 🔃

HAVE READY FOR HOT POT STOCK:
 2 cans clear chicken broth (skim off fat)
 2 cans water

PREPARE THIN-SLICED COOKING INGREDIENTS:
 1 bunch celery cabbage
  (wash, cut into four
  sections, remove
  hard core, then cut
  into thirds
  horizontally)
 ½ pound cellophane
  noodles (soak in
  warm water for
  30 minutes, then
  cut with kitchen
  scissors into
  3" lengths)
 4 squares fresh bean
  curd (cut each
  square into approxi-
  mately 12 pieces)
 1 pound New York cut
  of beef (have
  butcher slice paper-
  thin into 4" to 5"
  lengths)
 1 pound uncooked
  shrimp (size 16 to
  a pound, shell,

clean, devein, slice
  in half and dry on
  paper towels)
 2 uncooked chicken
  breasts (deboned,
  skinned and thin-
  sliced)
 ½ pound of filet of sole
  (thin-sliced into 3"
  lengths)
 ½ pound fresh spinach
  (wash carefully, cut
  off tough end of
  stem, leave whole)
 1 pound fresh squid,
  optional (cut off
  head, peel black
  skin from one side,
  remove backbone
  from the other
  side, then score
  with a knife and
  cut each squid
  into four pieces)

HAVE READY, FOR MASTER SAUCE (MILD):
 Combine in one bowl:
  1 cup Chinese dark soy sauce
  ½ cup thin Chinese soy sauce
  1 cup red wine vinegar
  ½ cup sesame oil
  1 tablespoon sugar (optional)

Additional condiments served on tray in separate sauce dishes:

6 unbroken eggs
(1 for each diner)

½ cup creamy peanut
butter

¼ cup minced garlic

½ cup chopped green
onion and stem

¼ cup fresh ginger root,
pared and minced

¼ cup Chinese chili
pepper sauce
(substitute Tabasco
sauce)

½ cup red cooking
sherry

TABLE SETTING:

Each guest should be provided with a Chinese rice bowl for his sauce, a dinner plate, soup spoon, one pair of chopsticks for dipping and an individual wire mesh strainer or slotted spoon.

Serves six guests generously.

Suggested Menus for Home Dining

FOR TWO:

Watercress Soup
Beef Pea Pods
Sweet & Sour Pork
White, Fried, or
   Chicken-fried Rice
Fresh Fruit
Tea

Sam See Soup
Almond Chicken
Sweet & Sour Shrimp
White or Pork-fried
   Rice
Fresh Fruit
Tea

Hot & Sour Soup
Barbecued Pork with
   Vegetables
Beef Pepper Steak
White, Fried or
   Shrimp-fried Rice
Fresh Fruit
Tea

Green Vegetable Soup
Wu's Beef
Lychee Chicken
White or Ham-fried
   Rice
Fresh Fruit
Tea

FOR FOUR:

(use ½ recipe ingredients
for each dish)

Green Vegetable Soup
Sliced Pork with
   Green & Red Peppers
Lemon Fish
Beef with Cauliflower
Sweet & Sour Shrimp
White Rice
Fresh Fruit
Tea

FOR SIX:

(increase all portions
by ¼)

Add Chicken with
   Plum Sauce

(use ½ recipe ingredients for each dish)	(increase all portions by ¼)
Fun See Soup	Add Lemon Fish
Beef with Black Bean Sauce	
Steam Chicken with Chinese Sausage	
Green Vegetable Soup	
Spinach with Bamboo Shoots	
Mushroom with Bean Curd	
Steamed Egg	
Cucumber Salad with Jellyfish	
Almond Delight with Mandarin Orange	

LUNCHEON OR BRIDGE PARTY BUFFET:

Tossed Shredded
  Chicken Salad
Wu's Beef
Sweet & Sour Shrimp
Chicken-fried Rice
Almond Delight
Tea

SIT-DOWN LUNCHEON PARTY:

Tossed Shredded
  Chicken Salad
Beef Pea Pods
Glass Shrimp with Peas
Lychee Chicken
White Rice
Fresh Fruit Bowl
Tea

DINNER FOR A
SPECIAL OCCASION:

Hot Appetizer Plate:
Diamond Shrimp
Balls, Crab Puffs,
Barbecued Beef,
Rumaki, Egg Rolls
Shark's Fin Soup
Peking Duck
Jade Chicken
Beef Oyster Sauce
Pea Pods with Black
Mushroom and
Water Chestnuts

Whole Sweet & Sour
Fish
Subgum Fried Rice
Eight Precious
Rice Cake
Tea
(If it's a birthday, add
a noodle dish.
Noodles signify long
life.)

— OR —

Sam See Soup
Beef Pepper Steak
Steamed Pork
Cashew Chicken
Sweet & Sour Shrimp
White or Pork-fried
Rice
Fresh Fruit

Tea

(for additional people,
increase all portions
by ¼)

Add Steamed
Egg Plant

COCKTAIL PARTY:

Appetizers: Shrimp
Toast, Crab Puffs
Barbecued Beef,
Fried Shrimp,
Rumaki, Egg Rolls or
Barbecued Spare
Ribs
Buffet Table: Almond
Chicken
Beef Oyster Sauce
Sweet & Sour Pork
Beef Lo Mein
Subgum Fried Rice
Cantonese Shrimp
with Black Bean
Sauce
Sweet & Sour Pork
Glass Shrimp with Peas
White or Chicken-fried
Rice
Fresh Fruit
Tea

VEGETARIAN DINNER:

Watercress Soup
Steamed Egg Plant
Chinese Mixed Greens
Buddha's Dish
Pea Pods with
Water Chestnuts
Hot & Sour String
Beans with
Carrots & Celery
White or Egg-fried
Rice
Fresh Fruit Bowl
or Glazed Banana
Tea

Now that you understand the methods of cooking, let me take you through the steps of giving your first dinner party for four persons (including yourself). I say four because the recipes in this book are planned for that number.

We will go step-by-step through the preparations and the actual cooking, each part taking about 30 minutes. We will select a menu that will afford a contrast in taste, texture and color sensations, and will include a soup, rice or noodles, two main dishes, dessert and tea. It should include a variety of cooking methods and no more than one or two quick-fry last-minute dishes. Here is a typical dinner party menu:

DISH	METHOD	MAIN INGREDIENT(S)
Fun See Soup	Boil-simmer	Chicken
White Boiled Rice	Boil-simmer	Rice
Beef with Pea Pods	Quick-fry	Beef-vegetable
Whole Sea Bass	Steam	Fish
Almond Delight	Chill	Gelatine
Tea		

First we will read through the recipes to be sure we have all the ingredients. Now we will determine the order in which preparations must be made, and the order of cooking. We are now ready to start preparations.

STEP 1: Soak Fun See (noodles) in cold water for 15 minutes, drain, cover, and store in refrigerator.

STEP 2: Thin-slice beef and place in marinade. Cover, store in refrigerator.

STEP 3: Bone, discard skin from chicken thigh, cut into strips for soup. Cover, store in refrigerator. Save bones for soup.

STEP 4: Dice Virginia ham, cover, refrigerate.

STEP 5: Wash, remove strings from pea pods, put in bowl, refrigerate.

STEP 6: Drain canned sliced water chestnuts. Put in bowl, cover, refrigerate.

The six steps should not have taken you more than half an hour. As you become accustomed to Chinese cooking, naturally you will become more efficient and faster, and you will be combining steps.

There is a short preparation time just before cooking, during which we will regard the recipes to determine the order of cooking (which dish takes longest to cook, which can be simmered until ready to serve, and which will have to be quick-fried just before serving).

Having determined this, we will assemble all the ingredients for each recipe, keeping them clustered separately; the first to be cooked placed closest to the stove. Any seasonings which can be combined and added together will be placed in a bowl. We will assemble all necessary utensils such as measuring cups, measuring spoons, spatulas, paper toweling and the like. Now we are ready to cook.

STEP 1: Boil rice, then allow it to simmer until ready to serve.

STEP 2: Boil soup to the point where you have added the chicken strips. Then cover and simmer until ready to add the Fun See and egg whites (minutes before serving).

STEP 3: Fill bottom of steamer with water, bring to a boil, add scored fish 8 to 10 minutes before serving.

STEP 4: Three minutes before serving, bring soup back to a boil. Add Fun See, cook for 2 minutes, then add eggs. Turn off heat. Cover.

STEP 5: Quick-fry the water chestnuts and pea pods. Put aside.

STEP 6: Quick-fry the marinated beef slices for 2 to 3 minutes. Add pea pod mixture, stir around, remove to serving dish.

STEP 7: Heat vegetable oil, pour over fish which is removed from steamer in its serving platter. Pour soy sauce over fish.

STEP 8: Seat guests.

STEP 9: Pour soup into tureen. Put rice into bowl. Serve on table.

STEP 10: Accept compliments graciously. Enjoy your own dinner party.

Leftover Dishes

Although we ate very well at home in China when I was a little girl, my grandfather trained us never to waste anything that was served on the table. He made this point in the following story.

"There was a rich man who always dined on sumptuous repasts of fish, chicken and meat. After a meal, what was not eaten was thrown away.

"Next door was another rich family. When the extravagant man threw out food, the neighbor would pick it up, wash it, dry it out to preserve it, then put it away.

"Eventually the rich man lost everything he had, and became so poor that he was forced to beg on the streets. But he stayed away from the street where he once lived because he did not want to be recognized. Eventually, driven by hunger, he swallowed his pride and went begging in front of the house of his former neighbor.

"The man came out with box after box of preserved foods. The beggar was most grateful and thanked him over and over again, finally asking, 'Why are you so good to me?'

The frugal neighbor said, 'Don't thank me, thank yourself. This is all the food you threw away and which I picked up and dried out.' "

The moral may be obvious to you. So, when you cook Chinese dishes, save your leftovers and use them in a number of the recipes I have given you in this book.

From infancy, the Chinese are taught never to waste food, not even a few grains of rice, and everything edible is saved to be used at another time. The average American refrigerator usually contains enough leftovers from which two or three additional meals can be made in the Chinese manner; so here are some suggestions on using the remains of yesterday's dishes for tonight's Chinese dinner. Recipes for all the dishes listed below are in this book.

ROAST BEEF: Beef with Cauliflower, Beef Asparagus with Black Bean Sauce, Beef with Chinese Cabbage, Beef Bean Curd, Beef Tomato.

PORK ROAST: Barbecued Pork with Chinese Vegetables, Sliced Pork with Red and Green Peppers, Sweet & Sour Pork.

HAM: Ham Fried Rice, Subgum Fried Rice, Ham Noodles in Broth (use ham instead of the pork I have listed in the pork recipe section).

CHICKEN: Tossed Shredded Chicken Salad, Lychee Chicken, Cantonese Chicken Chow Mein, Shanghai Chicken Salad, Chicken Oyster Sauce, Almond Chicken, Cucumber Salad with Chicken Shreds.

STEAK: Pepper Steak, Tomato Beef, Beef Lo Mein, Beef Oyster Sauce.

TURKEY: Turkey Congee, Turkey with Oyster Sauce.

Save all vegetables, fresh or cooked. As you progress in the art of Chinese cooking, you will find dozens of dishes in which you can put them to good use.

You will note that in this book I have not listed the leftover recipes in a separate section; instead they are included in the listing of the main leftover ingredient.

Chinese restaurateurs consider it a compliment when diners wish to take their leftovers home.

However, because of the number of different dishes in the usual Chinese meal, it can sometimes become a problem. At our restaurant we deliver the "doggie bags" directly to the cars of many of our regular patrons. The leftovers can then be frozen, replenished with some dishes made at home, and served as a full meal.

A Diet Program on Chinese Foods

There is an almost universal interest in diet and weight control, even in the consumption of Chinese foods which are generally reputed to be less fattening, so I have prepared a chart which shows the caloric value of the most commonly used Chinese ingredients.

I believe that proper weight reduction is a matter of personalized medical advice; there is no one good diet which is suitable for everyone. The diet must be well-balanced, with all the essential nutrients you require. If you're cooking at home and are counting calories, the following chart will, I trust, be of valuable aid to you.

CEREALS & GRAIN PRODUCTS

Flour (all-purpose)	1 cup	400 calories
Rice	4 oz.	180 calories
Rice (glutinous)	4 oz.	402 calories
Rice noodles (Chinese egg noodles)	4 oz.	288 calories
Vermicelli	4 oz.	288 calories

STARCHY ROOTS & STEMS

Water chestnut	4 oz.	73 calories
Sweet potato (red)	4 oz.	128 calories
Lotus root	4 oz.	59 calories

LEGUMES, SEEDS & NUTS

Lotus seeds	4 oz.	351 calories
Soy bean curd (cake)	4 oz.	74 calories
Soy bean	4 oz.	369 calories
Peanuts (chopped)	1 T.	50 calories
Almonds	12 nuts	100 calories
Cashews	¾ cup	578 calories
Chestnuts	8 nuts	50 calories
Almonds (toasted)	12 nuts	100 calories
Pecans	8 nuts	50 calories
Red beans	4 oz.	342 calories
Sesame seeds (white)	4 oz.	666 calories
Soy bean sauce	4 oz.	202 calories

OIL & FATS
Vegetable oil   1 cup   884 calories

DAIRY PRODUCTS
Egg (yolk)	4 oz.	395 calories
Egg (white)	4 oz.	55 calories
Cream cheese	1 oz.	105 calories
Thousand year egg	4 oz.	203 calories
Ginger ice cream	1 scoop	150 calories

MEAT & POULTRY PRODUCTS
Beef (lean)	4 oz.	151 calories
Beef (with fat)	4 oz.	301 calories
Pork (lean)	4 oz.	394 calories
Pork (medium)	4 oz.	624 calories
Pork (fat)	4 oz.	935 calories
Pork spare ribs	8 pcs. 3" each	250 calories
Pork kidney	4 oz.	130 calories
Boiled ham	4 oz.	350 calories
Bacon	3 strips	100 calories
Ham (Virginia)	4 oz.	270 calories
Chicken	4 oz.	132 calories
Chicken liver	4 oz.	150 calories
Turkey	4 oz.	250 calories
Squab	1 squab	150 calories
Duck	4 oz.	208 calories
Chinese sausage	4 oz.	504 calories

FISH & MARINE PRODUCTS
Abalone (canned)	4 oz.	91 calories
Abalone (dried)	4 oz.	351 calories
Abalone (raw)	4 oz.	122 calories
Shark's fin	4 oz.	428 calories
Crab meat	3½ oz.	104 calories
Lobster (fresh)	4 oz.	96 calories
Lobster (canned)	3½ oz.	92 calories
Shrimp (fresh)	4 oz.	99 calories
Shrimp (dried)	4 oz.	224 calories
Sea bass	4 oz.	110 calories
Red snapper	4 oz.	132 calories
Filet of sole	4 oz.	125 calories
Squid (fresh)	4 oz.	93 calories
Squid (dried)	4 oz.	305 calories

VEGETABLES
Winter melon   4 oz.   8 calories

Bamboo shoots	4 oz.	32 calories
Mushrooms (Chinese, black)	4 oz.	146 calories
Mustard pickles	4 oz.	32 calories
Pea pods	4 oz.	36 calories
Water cress	4 oz.	22 calories
Chinese greens (Pe-Tsai)	4 oz.	17 calories
Snow peas	4 oz.	36 calories
Button mushrooms	3½ oz.	16 calories
Cloud ear fungus	4 oz.	128 calories
Green onion	4 oz.	31 calories
Brussel sprouts	1 cup	60 calories
Cabbage	4 oz.	19 calories
Green pepper	1 large	25 calories
White onion	2½″ diameter	45 calories
Lettuce	4 oz.	16 calories
Turnips	⅔ cup diced	27 calories
Celery	1 stalk	15 calories
Garlic	4 oz.	108 calories
Ginger	4 oz.	42 calories
Seaweeds (agar agar)	4 oz.	211 calories
Bean sprouts	4 oz.	17 calories
Cream style sweet corn (canned)	⅔ cup	85 calories
Asparagus (yellow, canned)	½ cup	22 calories
Asparagus (fresh)	½ cup	20 calories
Cucumber	12 slices ⅛″ thick	12 calories
Parsley (chopped)	1 T.	1 calory
Red pepper	4 oz.	30 calories
Chinese broccoli	4 oz.	33 calories
American broccoli	1 med. stalk	29 calories
Green peas (fresh or frozen)	⅔ cup	70 calories
Tomato	1 small	20 calories
Cauliflower (buds)	1 cup	25 calories
Bitter melon (Balsam pear)	4 oz.	15 calories
Spinach	3½ oz.	20 calories
Eggplant	3 slices, 4″ diam.	24 calories
Carrots	2½″ x 1″	42 calories
Red cabbage	4 oz.	22 calories

FRUITS

Coconut (dried)	4 oz.	722 calories
Coconut (fresh)	4 oz.	408 calories
Pineapple (canned)	2 slices ½" thick	78 calories
Cherries	1 cup	95 calories
Lychee (dried)	4 oz.	315 calories
Lychee (fresh)	4 oz.	73 calories
Candied kumquats	4 oz.	74 calories
Seedless raisins	1 cup	450 calories
Candied orange peel	3½ oz.	316 calories
Dates (whole)	½ cup	250 calories
Apple	1 small	75 calories
Bananas	1 medium	100 calories

MISCELLANEOUS

Chicken broth	1 cup	100 calories
Cornstarch	1 T.	30 calories
Vinegar	4 oz.	12 calories
Sugar	1 tsp.	16 calories
Salt		0 calories
Wine (red)	1 claret glass	95 calories
Sherry	1 sherry glass	38 calories
Champagne	1 champagne glass	105 calories
Catsup	1 T.	25 calories
	or 4 oz.	106 calories
Lemon juice	1 T.	4 calories
Honey	1 T.	62 calories
Brown sugar	½ cup	370 calories

Chinese excellence in the art of cooking is partly attributable to the fact that wherever my ancestors lived, they made tasty dishes of whatever was available. If it was edible, they could prepare it in a most succulent way. This should be of great comfort to those of you who do not have a Chinatown, or an Oriental grocery store nearby, for Chinese cooking frees your imagination to substitute other ingredients.

Whether in the seasonings or in the main ingredients, throughout this chapter I have suggested substitutions for those items which might not be readily available to you. When no substitute is possible, such as bird's nest or shark's fin, none is listed.

I have included the phonetic spelling of each ingredient to help you in ordering at a Chinese market. I have also tried to suggest how best to store the ingredients. Here I would like to add that you must be scrupulously clean in transferring items from one container to another. For example, if you have opened a can of water chestnuts and are using just a portion of the contents, be sure the utensil with which you transfer them to a lidded jar is freshly washed and has not been used for anything else. This is to insure that no bacteria is on the utensils to cause the food to spoil.

Here is another example: as I have mentioned, the Chinese way of serving is to set all the cooked dishes on a lazy susan in the center of the dining table, and each person helps himself as often as he likes, transferring food from the dishes to his plate. We use a pair of serving chopsticks in each dish, and a pair for each diner. If there are leftovers to be transferred into another dish and placed in the refrigerator, we use a third set of freshly washed chopsticks.

When the articles are dried ingredients, they are merely kept in their packages in your pantry, and will last for long periods of time. Canned staples such as bamboo shoots, water chestnuts and others preserved in water are taken from the cans, rinsed in clear water and then placed in lidded jars filled with fresh water. The water must be changed every other day, and the contents will thus keep from three weeks to a month.

ABALONE

(Bao Yue) A large sea mollusk with a flattened, oval, slightly spiral shell, fresh or canned abalone should be cooked very little or it will become tough and rubbery. It is available in Chinese stores either dried or canned. I suggest the canned variety, which is cheaper than the dried, easier to prepare and saves time. To store, rinse in cold water, place in a covered jar in refrigerator. Lasts two weeks. A substitute is fresh scallops.

AGAR AGAR

(Dai Choi Goo) A gelatin extracted from red seaweed, sold in bulk or by package in Chinese stores in a dried, crinkly translucent form.

BAMBOO SHOOTS

(Juk Suhn) Ivory-colored, cone-shaped whole shoots of tropical bamboo, about four inches long, three inches in diameter. Canned, they come in four sizes: whole, diced, sliced and shredded. They are popular because of their crisp texture. To store, rinse and place in covered jar filled with water, refrigerate. Change water. Substitutes are kohlrabi or celery roots, for texture but not for flavor. Canned bamboo shoots are widely available in supermarkets.

BEAN CURD

(Dow Foo) It looks like a white cheesecake, about three inches square, one-half inch high. It is made by grinding softened soy beans with water into a milk which is coagulated into a soft cake. Bland, it mixes well with more highly seasoned foods. The vegetarian Buddhists call it "the meat without bones" because of its high protein content. It is inexpensive and can be eaten chilled, seasoned to taste with soy sauce and sesame oil, or it can be cooked. To store, cover with water, place in an open jar in the refrigerator. If water is changed daily, it will keep up to two weeks.

BEAN CURD SHEETS (DRIED)

(Dow Fu Pa) The sheets come in different sizes, but the most popular are the 24-inch diameter circles. When soy beans are put into large round vats to make the curd, a thin skin forms on the top. This skin, full of vitamins, is carefully removed and set in the sun to dry. Temple vegetarian monks use these bean curd sheets instead of meat.

BLACK BEANS

(Dow See) These are tiny oval black beans with a sharp, salty taste. Fresh, they must be washed well to get out the sand, then soaked. They are popularly mashed with garlic to use as a seasoning. They are also available canned, in Chinese stores. To store, dried in pantry; once soaked, they cannot be stored. A substitute is prepared Chinese bean sauce called Mein See.

BEANS, BROWN SAUCE

(Mein See) A thick brown sauce made from fermented soy beans, flour and salt, available in a one-pound tin or jar in Chinese groceries.

BEANS, RED (PASTE) (Hung Dow Sah) A thick, sweet paste made from red soy beans, used in desserts. Available in cans in Chinese stores. To store, refrigerate in a covered jar. Keeps for months.

BEANS, RED (Hung Dow) Tiny, smooth red beans used in soups and in pastes for sweet dishes. Sold by weight in Oriental markets.

BEAN SPROUTS (Ngah Choi) About two inches long, these are sprouts of the mung bean, widely used in Chinese restaurants, because they are inexpensive and easy to grow. If you are in a city with a Chinatown, be sure to visit the "factory" where bean sprouts are grown. To use, peel the strings off the top and bottom. Whenever I want to sit quietly and think, I gather a bowlful of fresh bean sprouts and de-string them. Very therapeutic. They are excellent in salad; blanch them for an instant in boiling water, then plunge into cold water and drain. I do not recommend canned or frozen sprouts. Substitutes can be shredded celery cabbage or the shredded heart of a lettuce head.

BEAN THREAD (Fun See) Also known as cellophane noodles, this thread-like white noodle is made from mung beans ground until thin, brittle and translucent. They come in two to six-ounce skeins that look like a nylon fishing line. They must be soaked in cold water before cooking. A substitute is very fine vermicelli.

BIRD'S NEST (Yeen Woh) This is actually a

swallow's nest of translucent gelatinous substance found on cliffs in isolated islands off Southeast Asia. It is harvested, dried and purified, and sold in see-through packages in Chinatown. There are two grades: the cheaper requires more cleaning and plucking out of bird's feathers and seeds. However, both must be cleaned meticulously and soaked overnight. Bird's nest is used mainly in soup for banquet fare in China. Rich in protein, the Chinese believe it adds to a woman's femininity and youthfulness. When I was sick as a child, my grandfather assigned one maid to sit in a chair near my bed not only to watch over me but also taking out the feathers from the bird's nest soup that was served to me daily for long weeks of my convalescence.

BROCCOLI, CHINESE (Gai Lan) A seasonal bright green vegetable with the texture but not the taste of American-type broccoli. It is quick-fried to retain its beautiful color and crisp texture. A substitute can be American broccoli.

CABBAGE, CHINESE (Bak Choi) It resembles celery, but has loose stalks with large, dark green leaves, about a foot long. The beginning Chinese cook may mistake its shape for celery. It cannot be eaten raw. A substitute is American cabbage.

CELERY CABBAGE, CHINESE (Sieu Choi) The shape of celery, but with stalks about four inches in diameter grown tightly together, ten to twelve inches long. The white stalks are tipped in light green. It can be eaten raw or quick-fried. A substitute is American cabbage.

CLOUD EAR (Wun Yee) A black, gelatinous fungus growing on trees which turns gray-brown when dried, changes to dark brown when soaked. It expands to several times its size. When cooked, it adds a crisp, crunchy texture to the dish. To store, after soaking, immerse in cold water in a covered jar in the refrigerator. Keeps for a week if the water is changed daily. A substitute is dried black mushrooms.

CORNSTARCH (Dow Fun) It is preferred over flour as a thickener because it looks clear and adds a sheen to ingredients. Added to batter, it gives a crisp texture to deep-fried foods. I prefer cornstarch to commercial meat tenderizers.

DATES, CHINESE (Hung Jo) These are dried jujubes, about the size of a marble; must be soaked overnight in cold water. Sold in cellophane packages by weight. Will keep indefinitely.

DRAGON'S EYE (Loong Gnon) A small fruit the size of a cherry, with a smooth but hard brown shell. Inside is a large dark pit with a pulpy grapelike fruit. Dragon's Eye can be bought dried without the shell for use in soups, or canned whole for desserts. A substitute is Chinese lychees.

EGGPLANT, ORIENTAL (Ai Gwa) It is longer and thinner than the American variety, but with fewer seeds. Most supermarkets carry them in season. A substitute is the American eggplant.

EGGS, DUCK (SALTED) (Hahm Dahn) Larger than hen's eggs, they are cured in black clay packing in brine for a month or more. To use, wash off the black clay and hard boil; shell and slice them as a side dish to be eaten with congee for breakfast, or shell and steam them with meat. They have a salty, tangy taste. To store, keep in black clay packing in pantry. After cooking, if shelled, keep covered in a bowl for two weeks in the refrigerator.

EGGS, THOUSAND-YEAR OLD (Pay Dahn) These are covered with paste of ashes, lime and salt, and buried for about 100 days. To be used, they must be washed, shelled and sliced. This petrified egg has a cheese-like flavor to the darkened yolk, while the egg white is a gelatinous-textured amber color. They are sliced for hors d'oeuvres or used in congee. Sold by the egg in Chinese markets. Also known as Hundred-Year-Old Eggs. To store, keep them in their box in the pantry. After shelling, store in the refrigerator for several weeks.

FIVE SPICE POWDER (Ng Heung Fun) A powdered blend of Chinese star anise, fennel, cinnamon, clove and Szechwan pepper. Used sparingly, it is sold by weight or box in Chinese stores. As a substitute, use all-spice powder, or a combination of ground cinnamon, clove, ginger, fennel and anise seed.

FUN SEE	(See BEAN THREAD)
GARLIC	(Seun Tao) A strong member of the onion family, bought as a dried bulb. In Chinese cooking, used mostly to add flavor to oil in quick-fry cooking, then discarded, or mashed with brown beans as a seasoning.
GINGER ROOT	(Sang Geong) A gnarled, beige-colored root about three inches long, with a yellowish beige inside. Used as a basic flavoring agent, it adds a delicate pungency to food and its strong aroma masks the seafood odor. When I use it in this manner, I always remove and discard the thin slice of ginger root before the dish is served. New ginger root shoots are thin-sliced and quick-fried with beef as a popular dish. Occasionally, the ginger root is minced fine and added to a dish. To store, keep in refrigerator; lasts about a month.
GOLDEN NEEDLE	(Gum Jum) It resembles a dried yellow flower called Tiger Lily, and is from two to three inches long. When softened in water before cooking, there is often a hard stem which should be cut off. Golden Needles have a light beef broth flavoring. Also known as Dried Lily Flower. To store, keep in pantry.
HAM, VIRGINIA	(Foh Toi) This is the closest to the "Golden Coin" ham of China which is no longer available. It is a cured smoked ham and can be bought by the slice in Chinese markets, gourmet shops and some supermarkets. To store, wrap in

foil, and place in the refrigerator for several weeks. Substitutes are Italian prosciutto or Westphalian ham.

HOISIN SAUCE (Hoi Sin Jeung) A thick, sweet, brownish-red sauce made from soy beans, flour, sugar and spices. It is sold in one-pound cans, or in larger amounts. To store, place the contents of the opened can in a lidded jar and keep refrigerated. Substitutes are Chinese plum sauce, or catsup and soy sauce mixed with a little sugar.

JELLYFISH (Hai Jit Pa) Dehydrated marine animal used as an ingredient in cold dishes. It has a bland taste but is a crisp texture. It must be soaked overnight and shredded.

KUMQUATS (Kumquat) Tiny, oval-shaped citrus fruit, dark tangerine in color, available in thick syrup, candied or fresh.

LYCHEES (Lychee) A small oval fruit with a large pit, white pulp and rough red skin. Seasonal, it can only be bought fresh in Chinese stores during the month of June. Otherwise it is canned. To store, place contents of can in a lidded jar and refrigerate. A substitute is Dragon's eyes.

LOTUS ROOT (Leen Ngow) Long tubular roots attached to each other like strings of sausage. The lotus root has a thin beige skin like a potato and the white inside has holes like swiss cheese, although symmetrical. It must be cooked before eating. It can be peeled, sliced and cooked as a vegetable;

or peeled, the holes stuffed with sweet paste, then steamed and sliced for a dessert. Sold in Chinese stores by sections, or canned or dried.

LOTUS SEEDS (Leen Gee) The size of a seedless grape, they have a brown skin and a hard brown tip. Inside they are white with a bitter green thread in the center. They must be soaked and the brown skin removed. I take a needle and push the bitter green thread out, and the seeds must be cooked until they are soft. Lotus seeds have no taste, they take on the flavor of whatever they are cooked with. I use the dried variety, but the canned, which are ready for cooking, would be simpler and faster to use. The are available in Chinese markets, dried or canned. Lotus seeds are a symbol of fertility, meaning a "successive birth of sons," so they are used in tea for weddings. The new bride serves her in-laws some lotus tea signifying (hopefully!) that her firstborn will be a son.

MELON, BITTER (Foo Gwa) Just as its name suggests, it is very bitter, the size of a cucumber, olive-green in color, with a bumpy surface. To prepare it for cooking, it must be sliced, seeds removed and then plunged into boiling water for an instant to remove some of the bitter taste. Then it is thin-sliced. I usually quick-fry it with garlic and black bean sauce. Available by weight in Chinese grocery stores.

MELON (Jik Gwa) It has the same color

and size of the bitter melon but has a rough surface and is tasteless. It is pared and the seeds removed, then usually stuffed with meat to be steamed, or cubed to be cooked in soup with pork. Available in Chinese markets. Zucchini is a substitute.

MUSHROOMS, BLACK

(Dung Goo) There are three main types of dried mushrooms: from the least to the most expensive they are (1) big but thin and least tender; (2) smaller but thicker, and (3) darker and thickest with large cracks in the surface. The third kind are called Flower Mushrooms and are the best for soup, since they have the finest flavor. For general cooking, I recommend the second type. Wash and rinse dried mushrooms before soaking them so that you can use the soaking liquid to flavor cooking—substitute the liquid whenever water is called for. I prefer to soak mushrooms overnight, but you can soften them in cold water in 20 minutes. Don't use hot water because it takes out too much flavor. Squeeze out the water before using the mushrooms.

MUSHROOMS, STRAW

(Chao Goo) Since world trade has opened with mainland China, straw mushrooms are being flown to Chinese grocers all over the world. In China, straw mushrooms are considered a delicacy. Shipped in 8-ounce cans, they look like a half-opened umbrella, and they have a smooth and tender texture.

NOODLES CELLOPHANE

(See FUN SEE)

NOODLES, CHINESE EGG

(Dahm Mein) Long, thin noodles about one-eighth of an inch wide, made from flour, eggs and water. They are sold by the pound, fresh or dried, in Chinese stores. Always have the water boiling before cooking noodles, then rinse in cold water and add a tablespoon of vegetable oil to give them a sheen and to keep them from sticking together. They are added to soup or meat dishes. To store, fresh noodles should be put in a plastic bag and kept in the refrigerator for one or two weeks. Any other thin egg noodles may be used as substitutes.

OYSTER SAUCE, CHINESE

(Ho Yao) The best kind is imported from Macao. It is a thick, brown sauce used for dipping or quick-frying. Reduce the amount of salt or soy sauce when oyster sauce is used. Comes in bottles or in cans. To store, pour contents of can into a lidded jar and refrigerate. Buy only a small amount at a time. Substitute is a mixture of juice from canned oysters, dark soy sauce, and a little catsup.

PARSLEY, CHINESE

(Yuen Sai) The same as coriander or Spanish cilantro, the leaves are more tender and it has a stronger flavor and aroma than the American variety. Can be bought in Chinese and Latin-American markets. Nearest substitute is Italian parsley for looks, but not for flavor or tenderness.

PEA PODS, CHINESE

(Snow Peas—Lahn Dow) Pale green flat pea pods with very small peas inside. Entire pod is tender and edible. They are

seasonal and the price fluctuates
from 70¢ a pound to $4.00.
Strings should be removed before
cooking. To store, keep in
refrigerator crisper but use as soon
as possible because pea pod
crispness fades rapidly. Fresh,
tender young string beans can be
used as a substitute.

**PEPPERS, FRESH
RED OR GREEN
LONG HOT** — (Ching Lat Jue) Refrigerate and
use sparingly. They are hot!

**PEPPERCORNS,
SZECHWAN** — (Far Jue) Looks like black
peppercorn, but is reddish-brown
and has a seed in the center. To
make seasoned salt, heat 3
tablespoons Szechwan
peppercorns in a dry wok. Cook,
shaking, until they start to smoke.
Either grind them in a blender or
pound with a mallet until
pulverized. Add 3 tablespoons
salt and blend.

PLUM SAUCE — (Suhn Mui Jeung) A reddish-
brown thick sauce with a sweet
and pungent flavor, made from
plum, apricot, chili, vinegar and
sugar. Widely used as a dip for
roast duck. Sold in cans and
bottles in Chinese stores. Add
sugar if it is too tart for your
taste. To store, transfer to covered
jar and it will keep for months in
the refrigerator. Substitute is apple
sauce mixed with a little sugar
and cider vingear, plus a bit of
catsup to give it color. Also
known as Duck Sauce.

RADISH, WHITE — (Loh Baak) A member of the
turnip family, it varies from six to
ten inches in length. It has a tan
skin, with a crisp white inside and

a sharp, piquant taste. Good when used raw in salads, and when cooked in soup, the Chinese regard it as a good medicine for a cold. Available in Oriental markets. Turnip is a substitute.

RICE, GLUTINOUS (Noh Mai) The size of long-grain rice but round in shape. Very soft and sticky when boiled. Sold by weight in Chinese stores, glutinous rice is used in ceremonial dishes and mostly for desserts such as Eight Precious Rice Pudding. My favorite way of preparing this rice is to cook it with Chinese sausage as a stuffing for roast turkey or duck.

RICE FLOUR, GLUTINOUS (Noh Mai Fun) This is a rice powder ground from glutinous rice used in sweet dishes and some meat dishes. Sold by weight.

RICE STICKS (Mai Fun) Thin, chalk-white noodles like cellophane noodles except for a different texture. They can be deep-fried; if not, they must be boiled before adding to cooked dishes. Available by package in Chinese markets. Cellophane noodles are a substitute.

SAUSAGE, CHINESE (Lop Cheong) Cured, highly spiced pork sausage hung in bunches in Chinese markets. Chinese sausage is steamed whole over rice until the fat is translucent, or it is thin-sliced and quick-fried. To store, it keeps like ham in your refrigerator. Ham is a substitute.

SCALLIONS (Tsung Choi) We use the white bulb and about six inches of the green stem. Scallions are often used with ginger root as a seasoning. When flavoring a dish, they are often tied into a knot with their own stem, then discarded before serving. They are also minced and used as a garnish, or cut into little brooms and served with duck. Available in all stores. The same as green onions.

SEAWEED, DRIED (Gee Choi) It is known as the "paper vegetable." Sold in dehydrated form in Oriental stores, it is paper-thin and black-purple. Excellent for use in soups.

SESAME SEEDS (Gee Mah) There are two kinds of these tiny flat seeds, black or white. Black sesame seeds are said in China to promote your hair growth. They are used in desserts, and the imported variety are available in many supermarkets.

SESAME SEED OIL (Gee Mah Yao) An amber-colored oil from roasted sesame seeds with a delightful nutty flavor. Just a few drops added to a salad or a bland dish will perk up the flavor. When adding sesame oil to a dish being cooked, add it at the very last and immediately take from the stove because heat destroys its delicate essence. Imported from China, it is sold in bottles in Chinese markets. It keeps indefinitely in the pantry.

SHARK'S FIN (Yu Chee) Translucent, thread-like dried cartilage from shark's fins. Very expensive, it is sold in Chinese markets and varies in quality as well as price. It is a gelatinous substance high in calcium content and is considered to be good for a man's virility. Shark's Fin Soup is always served at banquets and festivals.

SHRIMP, DRIED (Har Mai) Tiny dried shrimp, amber-colored, they have a sharp, salty taste. Sold by weight in Oriental stores.

SOY SAUCE (See Yao) A piquant, salty brown liquid made from fermented soy beans, wheat flour, salt, yeast and water. The imported Chinese and Japanese soy sauces are the best. They vary from a thin to a thick density, in color from light brown and saltier, to a dark reddish-brown used more for color than for adding a salty tang. Not quite a substitute, but I prefer to use two different Chinese varieties of soy sauce at the same time to get just the right taste, but if you are not near a Chinese market, you can substitute the Japanese soy sauce.

STAR ANISE (Bat Gok) This licorice-flavored spice in a burnt-sienna color looks like a tiny eight-pointed star, between an inch and a half-inch in width. Sold in Chinese markets, For a substitute, use a sparing amount of anise powder, preferable to anise seed.

SZECHWAN PEPPER (Fagara) Brown peppercorns with an extremely hot flavor. Sold by weight in Chinese stores when it is available. Black peppercorns are a substitute.

WATER CHESTNUTS (Mah Tai) A dark brown bulb packed in mud to keep it from drying out and spoiling. Wash off the mud pack, peel and cut to the shape you want. They are eaten raw like a fruit in China. Although cooked water chestnuts are available in cans, they do not have quite as good a taste as the fresh chestnuts. To store the canned variety, pour the liquid out, rinse water chestnuts in clear water, cover with water and store in a covered jar in the refrigerator. If you change the water every other day, they will last about a month.

WINTER MELON   (**Dung Gwa**) The size of a medium watermelon, about the same green color but with an overlay of frosty white, it is sold whole or by the slice in Chinese markets and is used mainly for soups. The meat is white, with little brown seeds. To prepare, pare the skin, scrape out the seeds, then slice or cut into chunks to cook. Another use of this melon is to fill it with a soup stock and steam it whole (see recipe).

WON TON   (**Won Tun Pae**) A dough made from flour, water and eggs, it is formed into squares for won ton or spring rolls. About three inches square, they are sold in Chinese markets or noodle factories by weight. They are filled and cooked in boiling water, or used for deep-frying. To store, keep in a freshly clean, wet towel for four or five days in the refrigerator. After that they lose their texture and become stiff.

Where to Buy Chinese Ingredients

(Companies with mailing service are marked with an asterisk*)

CALIFORNIA

Yee Sing Chong Co.
960 North Hill St.
Los Angeles, Calif. 90012

Kwong Dack Wo Co.
702 North Spring St.
Los Angeles, Calif. 90012

Kwong On Lung
680 North Spring St.
Los Angeles, Calif. 90012

Wing Chong Lung Co.*
922 S. San Pedro St.
Los Angeles, Calif. 90015

Kwong On Teong
720 Webster St.
Oakland, Calif. 94607

Wing Chong Co.
367 Eighth Street
Oakland, Calif. 94607

Mow Lee Sing Kee Co.*
730 Grant Avenue
San Francisco, Calif. 94108

Gim Fat Co., Inc.
953 Grant Avenue
San Francisco, Calif. 94108

Moon John
830 Grant Avenue
San Francisco, Calif. 94108

Wing Sing Chong Co.
1076 Stockton Street
San Francisco, Calif. 94108

Mow Lee Shing Kee Co.*
774 Commercial St.
San Francisco, Calif.

Yick Chong Co.
423 "J" Street
Sacramento, Calif. 95831

DISTRICT OF COLUMBIA

Mee Wah Lung Co.
608 H Street N.W.
Washington, D.C. 20001

Tuck Cheong & Co.
716 H Street N.W.
Washington, D.C. 20001

New China Supply Co.
709 H Street N.W.
Washington, D.C. 20001

ILLINOIS

Kam Shing Co.*
2246 S. Wentworth St.
Chicago, Ill. 60616

China Farms
733 West Randolph St.
Chicago, Ill.

MASSACHUSETTS

Sun See Co.
36 Harrison Avenue
Boston, Mass. 02111

Chung Lung
18 Hudson Street
Boston, Mass.

T. H. Lung
9 Hudson Street
Boston, Mass.

Sun Sun
34 Oxford Street
Boston, Mass.

Wing Wing
79 Harrison Avenue
Boston, Mass.

NEW YORK
Oriental Food Shop*
1032 Amsterdam Avenue
New York, N.Y. 10027

Wing Woh Lung
50 Mott Street
New York, N.Y. 10013

Mon Fong Wo Co.*
36 Pell Street
New York, N.Y. 10013

Wo Fat Co.
16 Bowery
New York, N.Y. 10013

PENNSYLVANIA
Wing On Grocery Store*
1005 Race Street
Philadelphia, Penn. 19107

TEXAS
Oriental Import-Export
    Co.
2009 Polk Street
Houston, Texas 77003

OREGON
Fong Chong Co.
301 N.W. Fourth Ave.
Portland, Oregon

WASHINGTON
Wah Young Co.
416 Eighth Avenue South
Seattle, Washington

Chinese Fortunes

Some wives don't get mad, they get even.

No one has ever loved anyone the way everyone wants to be loved.

Everything is not yet lost.

Opportunity knocks only once. Be alert.

Every man is the architect of his own fortune.

What the eye does not see, the heart does not grieve for.

What is done cannot be undone.

Take time to love and be loved, it is a god-given privilege.

Better to be alone than in bad company.

Use or submit to authority with grace and philosophy.

Don't let your time disappear without a gain.

Concern yourself with getting enough rest and dollars.

You are doomed to be happy in wedlock.

A surprise message may loom in your emotional life.

Work with as little strain as possible, wait for a fortune.

You sense that there are big things ahead. Celebrate.

Mental work is your best asset, but don't go to extremes.

Romance and pleasure lie close at hand.

Be frank; let others know exactly where you stand.

Watch your money as it tends to run through your fingers.

Take some of the acid from your speech.

Don't abuse love; it can be preserved only by kindness.

You are regarded as a stepping stone by old friends.

Confine your social life to your free hours.

Keep impulses along lines that don't undermine essentials.

Early hours are dangerous because of over-optimism.

A valuable suggestion will make your job much easier.

You will gain your object by force of your own will power.

A short trip will bring you in contact with important people.

Watch your expenditures and check any tendency to waste.

Find harmony among family and friends, be content.

It will be better not to write the letter you planned.

Work hard but in a temperate manner.

You may have to assume new authority. Be ready.

You will meet a future friendship at a party.

Late hours bring excellent social contacts and more friends.

Exercise judgment in connection with things at hand.

If there's anything you want involving others, ask for it.

Trend to wasted energy should be stopped.

Your romantic life is interesting only to you.

You're all geared up and need rest and relaxation.

Be sure you aren't led into unsound business ventures.

A legend gets started easily and there is no way to stop it.

Efficiency enables you to end year with sense of fulfillment.

Check yourself before you do anything hasty.

Local gossip is unreliable. Be detached, remote.

Do the things you like for greater satisfaction.

Increase the size of personal letters you write next week.

Look afar and see the end from the beginning.

Jealousy and competition will trouble you.

News of an old sweetheart who still thinks of you.

You are a real leader rather than a follower.

Advancement you seek may be close at hand.

Talent, like the gout, sometimes skips two generations.

A wealthy person may make your home like a paradise.

Sincerity and tenderness will add happiness in your home.

Restore good feelings by taking an objective view.

By a stroke of good luck you may receive a bonus.

Get off to a new start, come out of your shell.

Putting things off is robbing yourself of chance.

You might be in love but don't be too hasty.

These are all suggestions. Writing your own
Chinese fortunes can be lots of fun.
Put them in a bowl and have each guest pick his own.

Use of M.S.G.

A Chinese cooking ingredient which is somewhat controversial is the taste powder called M.S.G., an abbreviation for monosodium glutamate. In earlier days it was processed from glutamic acid extracted from edible seaweed, but in the 1920s a Chinese scientist developed M.S.G. from wheat protein.

The most popular commercial brand is marketed as Ac'cent. Monosodium glutamate is tasteless itself, but the use of a very small portion of it brings out subtle flavors of such bland ingredients as chicken and certain vegetables.

Whenever I have listed it in a recipe, you will note that I suggest only a few grains; and for those who might be allergic to it, I have indicated its use as optional.

The use of M.S.G. was criticized in a recent article in the Wall Street Journal. However, I think the fault is in its overuse, not in the seasoning itself. Perhaps a few chefs subscribe to the theory that if a little will help, a lot will cure.

If you feel thirsty after coming home from a Chinese restaurant, chances are the chef was over-enthusiastic in using M.S.G. When I have had this experience, the next time I have asked that it be used more sparingly. I'd suggest you do the same.

Wines

I frankly admit that I am not an expert on wines; my comments and suggestions come from observing what the patrons of my restaurant seem to prefer.

Unless you have a connoisseur at your table, there are really no hard and fast rules for serving wines with your Chinese dinner. The general rules for using wines with Chinese foods are similar to those for most American and continental dishes: white wine with fish or fowl, red wine with meat.

Most native Chinese wines are made from rice and are served in a warmer, similar to the Japanese beverage, sake. Serving a Chinese wine may be an interesting novelty, but I have found that it requires a specially developed taste to truly enjoy and recommend that you have more familiar table wines available. If you wish to try a Chinese wine, Shao Hsing is most popular.

Wan Fu is a wine that is also very popular with gourmets of Chinese food. Curiously enough, it is bottled in France and is a light white wine which seems to go well with most dishes. Its name means "a million blessings."

I particularly enjoy a Beaujolais with my meal (as does Cary Grant), and this warm, zestful burgundy always seems to dress up a dinner party or banquet table.

California wines are most popular in my restaurant, and find that from the standpoint of variety, quality and cost they have earned their popularity. White pinot and chenin blanc go splendidly with fowl and fowl dishes and particularly well with mo goo gai pan and shredded chicken salad. Pinot chardonay is excellent with sizzling go ba or minced squab.

In China, red wine is a color for happy occasions, so you will see red wines served at weddings, birthday parties, christenings and banquets. I would also serve a red wine with duck and lobster Cantonese.

You might try serving wine in small wine cups instead of regular wine glasses. It seems to add to the special atmosphere and encourage conversation during the meal.

Index

ABOUT THE AUTHOR

MADAME SYLVIA WU, the daughter of a wealthy merchant, came to the United States with her family from Kiukiang, China, during World War II. She married a young M.I.T. engineering student, King Yan Wu, whose grandfather Dr. T. F. Wu was co-founder of the Republic of China with Dr. Sun Yat Sen. After her three children were in school, she opened Madame Wu's Garden in Santa Monica. Her restaurant is a gathering place of names and faces which are easily recognized; on any evening, such familiar faces as Mae West, Cary Grant, Bob Hope, Robert Redford, Dinah Shore and Johnny Carson might be seen in the dining rooms. Madame Wu also conducts her popular Thursday night cooking classes in the Dynasty Room. It was because of these classes that she was able to prepare her cookbook. She conducted a series of fifty-two individual classes, testing the dishes in portions for four people, and it required two years of recording, adding material and editing to complete the writing of her book.

KITCHEN POWER!

☐	11107	**MICHEL GUERARD'S CUISINE MINCEUR** Michel Guerard	$2.50
☐	2708	**COOKING WITHOUT A GRAIN OF SALT** Elma Bagg	$1.95
☐	11782	**ART OF FISH COOKERY** Milo Milorandovich	$1.75
☐	2965	**THE ROMAGNOLIS' TABLE** Romagnolis	$1.95
☐	6499	**BETTER HOMES & GARDENS COOKING FOR TWO**	$1.25
☐	8667	**BETTY CROCKER'S GOOD AND EASY COOKBOOK**	$1.50
☐	8809	**THE WORLD-FAMOUS RATNER'S MEATLESS COOKBOOK** Judy Gethers	$1.50
☐	10157	**THE BETTER HOMES & GARDENS BARBECUE BOOK**	$1.50
☐	10168	**THE COMPLETE BOOK OF MEXICAN COOKING** Elisabeth Ortiz	$1.50
☐	10348	**THE FRENCH CHEF COOKBOOK** Julia Child	$2.25
☐	12107	**WHOLE EARTH COOKBOOK** Cadwallader & Ohr	$1.95
☐	10468	**BLEND IT SPLENDID: THE NATURAL FOODS BLENDER BOOK** Dworkins	$1.50
☐	10532	**BETTER HOMES & GARDENS CALORIE COUNTER'S COOKBOOK**	$1.50
☐	10805	**BETTY CROCKER'S DINNER FOR TWO**	$1.50
☐	11188	**BETTY CROCKER'S DINNER PARTIES**	$1.50
☐	11299	**THE SPANISH COOKBOOK** Barbara Norman	$1.50
☐	11377	**CREPE COOKERY** Mable Hoffman	$1.95

Buy them at your local bookstore or use this handy coupon for ordering:

Bantam Books, Inc., Dept. KP2, 414 East Golf Road, Des Plaines, Ill. 60016

Please send me the books I have checked above. I am enclosing $_____
(please add 50¢ to cover postage and handling.) Send check or money order
—no cash or C.O.D.'s please.

Mr/Mrs/Miss_____

Address_____

City_____State/Zip_____

KP2—5/78

Please allow four weeks for delivery. This offer expires 11/78.

KITCHEN POWER!

☐ 12207	**COOKING WITH HERBS AND SPICES** Craig Claiborne	$2.50
☐ 11371	**SOURDOUGH COOKERY** Rita Davenport	$1.95
☐ 10486	**MASTERING MICROWAVE COOKING** Scotts	$1.95
☐ 2030	**PUTTING FOOD BY** Hertzberg, Vaughan & Greene	$2.50
☐ 2220	**AMERICAN HERITAGE COOKBOOK**	$1.95
☐ 11888	**CROCKERY COOKERY** Mable Hoffman	$2.25
☐ 6482	**ORIENTAL COOKING** Myra Waldo	$1.25
☐ 8064	**THE COMPLETE BOOK OF PASTA** Jack Denton Scott	$1.25
☐ 12241	**MADAME WU'S ART OF CHINESE COOKING**	$1.95
☐ 12186	**BETTER HOMES & GARDENS HOME** **CANNING COOKBOOK**	$1.95
☐ 10477	**BETTY CROCKER'S COOKBOOK**	$2.25
☐ 10538	**AMERICA'S FAVORITE RECIPES FROM** **BETTER HOMES & GARDENS**	$1.50
☐ 10539	**BETTER HOMES & GARDENS CASSEROLE COOKBOOK**	$1.50
☐ 12309	**THE ART OF FRENCH COOKING** Fernande Garvin	$1.75
☐ 12199	**THE ART OF JEWISH COOKING** Jennie Grossinger	$1.95
☐ 12316	**THE ART OF ITALIAN COOKING** Mario LoPinto	$1.75

Buy them wherever Bantam Bestsellers are sold or use this handy coupon:

Bantam Book Catalog

Here's your up-to-the-minute listing of every book currently available from Bantam.

This easy-to-use catalog is divided into categories and contains over 1400 titles by your favorite authors.

So don't delay—take advantage of this special opportunity to increase your reading pleasure.

Just send us your name and address and 25¢ (to help defray postage and handling costs).